MITHAI

TARLA DALAL
India's #1 Cookery Author

SANJAY & CO.
BOMBAY

Sixth Printing 2006

ISBN : 81-86469-38-9

Price : **Rs. 230/-**

Published & Distributed by :

SANJAY & COMPANY,

353/A-1, Shah & Nahar Industrial Estate, Dhanraj Mill Compound,

Lower Parel (W), Mumbai - 400 013. INDIA. Tel. : (91-22) 2496 8068.

Fax : (91-22) 2496 5876 E-mail : sanjay@tarladalal.com

Recipe Research &	**Photography**
Production Design	VINAY MAHIDHAR
PINKY CHANDAN	
ARATI FEDANE	**Food Styling**
JYOTI SHROFF	NITIN TANDON
Designed by	**Printed by**
S. KISHOR	MINAL SALES AGENCIES, MUMBAI

OTHER BOOKS
BY TARLA DALAL

INDIAN COOKING
Tava Cooking
Rotis & Subzis
Desi Khana
The Complete Gujarati Cook Book
Chaat
Achaar aur Parathe
The Rajasthani Cookbook
Swadisht Subzian

WESTERN COOKING
The Complete Italian Cookbook
The Chocolate Cookbook
Eggless Desserts
Mocktails & Snacks
Soups & Salads
Mexican Cooking
Easy Gourmet Cooking
Chinese Cooking
Easy Chinese Cooking
Thai Cooking
Sizzlers & Barbeques

TOTAL HEALTH
Low Calorie Healthy Cooking
Pregnancy Cookbook
Baby and Toddler Cookbook
Cooking with 1 Teaspoon of Oil
Home Remedies
Delicious Diabetic Recipes
Fast Foods Made Healthy
Healthy Soups & Salads
Healthy Breakfast
Calcium Rich Recipes
Healthy Heart Cook Book
Forever Young Diet
Healthy Snacks
Iron Rich Recipes
Healthy Juices
Low Cholesterol Recipes
Good Food for Diabetes
Healthy Subzis
Healthy Snacks for Kids
High Blood Pressure Cook Book
Low Calorie Sweets New
Nutritious Recipes for Pregnancy New

GENERAL COOKING
Exciting Vegetarian Cooking
Microwave Recipes
Quick & Easy Cooking
Saatvik Khana
Mixer Cook Book
The Pleasures of Vegetarian Cooking
The Delights of Vegetarian Cooking
The Joys of Vegetarian Cooking
Cooking with Kids
Snacks Under 10 Minutes
Ice-Cream & Frozen Desserts
Desserts Under 10 Minutes
Entertaining
Microwave Snacks & Desserts

MINI SERIES
Idlis & Dosas
Cooking under 10 minutes
Pizzas and Pasta
Fun Food for Children
Roz Ka Khana
Microwave - Desi Khana
T.V. Meals
Paneer
Parathas
Chawal
Dals
Sandwiches
Quick Cooking
Curries & Kadhis
Chinese Recipes
Jain Desi Khana
7 Dinner Menus
Jain International Recipes
Punjabi Subzis
Corn
Microwave Subzis New

INTRODUCTION

MITHAIS, also known as "Mishtaan" (meaning sweet food), are synonymous with celebrations in India. Any good news be that of a promotion, marriage, birth in a family or the like is invariably heralded with a box of sweets. Our favourite expression is "muh meetha karo".

An astounding variety of sweets is available from different parts of the country. This culinary heritage which has been passed down from generation to generation needs to be preserved. There are many times one wishes to have some knowledge of this culinary expertise to make something special and appropriate for the occasion. In this book, I have listed step-by-step instructions for recipes which will enable you to make your favourite sweets easily at home. The list includes Bengali sweets like rasgullas, chum chum, raj bhog, milk and mava based sweets and of course, the favourite sandesh, to name a few.

There lots of sweets one can make from the basic rasgulla, sandesh and dry fruit based mithais. I have suggested a few but there should be no end to one's creativity and you can always create something new using these basic recipes. Also one can buy rasgullas from a sweet shop and garnish them to create a completely new mithai, but this should be only to save on time as there is nothing quite as rewarding as home-made rasgullas!

There are also certain recipes which have sugarless or sugar free options where I have used the natural sweetness of the ingredients like dates or honey and there are some which use artificial sweeteners. Use your discretion when using these as they may not be suitable for all people.

Certain intricate sweets may take a little practice and experience like Mysore Pak and Ghevar. But do not be disheartened as there are several recipes ideal for beginners as well. Mithais are actually quite easy to prepare as you will find out yourself and once you have mastered the techniques of making these scrumptious delicacies at home, you would hardly need to go to a sweet shop.

Have fun with these recipes!

Happy cooking,

GLOSSARY

GHEE

Ghee or clarified butter is the purest form of butter or fat. The fragrance of fresh ghee is powerful and suffuses the house. Now-a-days, ghee is available commercially packed in metal cans or plastic packs. Although commercially packed ghee is very good, it loses some of its original flavour because of intensive processing.

To make ghee, full cream milk is converted into curds or yoghurt. This is then churned to separate out the solid BUTTER from the liquid (buttermilk). This butter is then placed in a heavy bottomed pan or kadai and melted. It is simmered to separate milk solids (which settle to the bottom of the pan) from the clear golden ghee. This ghee is then strained into a metal or glass jar and cooled completely.

Ghee is used in the making of mithai because of its flavour. It is also easier to digest than oil or vanaspati.

VANASPATI

Vanaspati is hydrogenated vegetable oil. It is an economical alternative to ghee and is widely available at most provision stores.

EDIBLE SILVER LEAF (VARQ)

Edible silver leaf is added as a garnish over sweets and can be seen shimmering in the glass cases of any sweet shop. Silver foil is as thin as the best chiffon. It is extremely fragile and often breaks up during use. It has no aroma or taste. It is sold between sheets of tissue paper. In the past, varq was made by continuously beating thin silver sheets between two layers of leather . However, now with the advent of new machinery, leather is no longer used to make varq.

CHENNA

This basic ingredient for Bengali sweets is made using only cow's milk. To make chenna, the milk is curdled and then strained through a muslin cloth to drain out the whey. This process is very similar to that of paneer, the difference being that for paneer there is an additional step where the curdled and strained milk is placed under a weight to enable all the whey to drain out. Chenna thus has more water content and a much looser texture as compared to paneer.

The quality of chenna depends largely on the quality of milk used. Good chenna is white in colour, has a neutral taste and a very smooth texture. Always ensure that fresh chenna is used in the preparation of the sweets. I have included a recipe for chenna in this book on page 128 which is easy to follow.

KHOYA (MAVA)

This is prepared by boiling milk in a broad non-stick pan and reducing it to a semi-solid stage. There are two types of khoya depending upon the type of milk used and the moisture content in the finished product.

1. Sada Khoya (Mava) : Also called "Batti ka Khoya", it is made of full fat milk. It has a very low moisture content and is used to make barfis and laddus. You will find the recipe on page 132.
2. Hariyali Khoya (Hariyali Mava) : Also called "Chikna Khoya", it is made with low fat milk. It is slightly yellowish in colour and is loose and sticky in consistency. It has a higher moisture content than the sada khoya and is used to make gulab jamuns.

SAFFRON

Saffron is the dried stigma of the saffron crocus plant. It is made up of fine, orange gold threads that are so light that 7,50,000 hand picked strands yield only about 450 grams.

Pure saffron is believed to be able to colour and flavour 70,000 times its weight in liquid.

It is the most expensive spice in the world due to its scarcity, fragility and flavour. Saffron is sold loosely matted like a lace of dark amber strands.

Saffron enhances savoury as well as sweet food. A few strands soaked in a little warm water or milk and added along with the liquid to the dish add a fragrant richness. It especially complements milk desserts and rice dishes like biryani .

ALUM

Commonly called "Phitkari", alum is translucent in appearance and is available both as loose crystals and small solid blocks. Alum is very versatile and is used as an antiseptic (for cuts and nicks), as a water purifier (it makes solid impurities settle at the bottom of the container) and also to curdle milk as in the recipe of **milk cake.**

SLAKED LIME

It is white in colour and has a chalky appearance. Slaked lime is commonly called chuna and it is one of the ingredients for paan which is relished all over India. The famous Agra delicacy, **petha** gets its characteristic crispness because of use of slaked lime.

MILK

Milk makes a very valuable contribution to the diet, being rich in protein, vitamins, calcium and other minerals. It is, in fact, the most complete single food we know of for vegetarians.

The different varieties of milk used in this book are :

1. **Full Fat Milk/ Whole Milk / Full Cream Milk**

   As the name indicates, this has a high fat content and is used to make rabdi, khoya, ice-cream etc. Now-a-days, full fat ultra heat treated (U.H.T.) milk, which has a longer shelf-life, is available in tetra-packs.

2. **Cow's Milk**

   This has a low fat content. It is used to make chenna which is the basic ingredient in various Bengali sweets and also in the preparation of hariyali khoya.

3. **Dried Milk / Milk Powder / Powdered Milk**

   It is spray dried whole milk to which vegetable fat is added. Water is evaporated from the milk by heat to produce solids. Powdered milk is packed in air-tight containers or vaccum packs and has a long shelf life. It can be reconstructed by dissolving it in water.

4. **Skimmed Milk Powder / Skim Milk Powder**

   It is the same as dried milk, the only difference being that it is spray dried skimmed milk instead of whole milk and is therefore is low in fat. It can be substituted in recipes in which whole milk powder is used.

PISTACHIO

Pistachio nuts are available in their shelled or unshelled form. The shells split neatly into two halves exposing a fresh apple-green nut streaked with violet. Pistachio nuts have virtually no aroma but they possess a rich, smooth, almost creamy taste.

To get a deep green coloured pistachio barfi, always use the "kishori" variety of pistachios which are smaller in size and brighter in colour.

TO MAKE SUGAR SYRUP

1. Place the sugar in a clean heavy bottomed pan. Use good quality sugar and add the specified quantity of water.

2. Place the pan over medium heat and allow the sugar to dissolve while stirring continuously.

3. Allow the syrup to simmer till it thickens slightly. If it coats the back of a spoon and trickles down in a thick stream, touch it with your index finger and press it between your thumb and index finger. On parting, one small string should form. This is a syrup of **1 string consistency**. It is used for making gulab jamuns, jalebis, dry fruit barfis etc.

4. To make a syrup of **2 string consistency**, simmer the syrup for a little longer and on repeating the same test, you should be able to obtain a stronger thread that is also longer than that of the one string consistency. On cooling slightly, you can obtain 2 to 3 threads that stay firm for longer. This is used to make sweets like mohanthaal, Mysore pak etc.

5. To make **Caramel** for chiki, all the water has to evaporate. The sugar will then start to caramalise and turn golden brown in colour. When it is light brown in colour, it is ready to be used to make chiki. For this, the sugar syrup has to be heated to 151°C to 160°C (302°F to 325°F). Caramel tends to colour and burn quickly so give it your full attention and remove it from the fire as soon as it turns golden brown in colour.

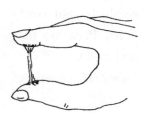 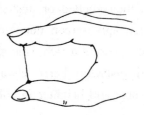 

INDEX

BARFIS, MILK & MAVA BASED MITHAI

SUGAR FREE MITHAIS

EASY SANDESH

BASIC RECIPES

RASGULLA MAGIC

RASGULLA

The famous Bengali sweet with its history of more than a century has crossed the boundaries of culture, caste and creed. It is relished almost everywhere in India and has been popularised abroad as well.

Preparation time : 30 mins.   Cooking time : 40 mins.
Makes 16 rasgullas.

FOR THE RASGULLAS
1 recipe chenna, page 128
1 teaspoon plain flour (maida) for dusting

FOR THE SUGAR SYRUP
5 cups sugar
½ cup milk

OTHER INGREDIENTS
2 teaspoons plain flour (maida)

FOR THE RASGULLAS
1. Divide the chenna into 16 equals parts and roll each part into a ball, taking care to see that the there are no cracks on the surface.
2. Dust the back of a flat plate (thali) lightly with the flour and place the rolled chenna balls on it.

FOR THE SUGAR SYRUP
1. Combine the sugar and milk with 3 cups of water in a large pan approx. 200 mm. (8") in diameter and 150 mm. (6") in height and heat while stirring continuously till the sugar dissolves. When the syrup comes to a boil, the impurities in the sugar will begin to float on the surface, forming a grey layer.

2. Heat over a medium flame to allow the grey layer to float. Do not stir at this point as the layer will break and it will not clarify the syrup.

3. After about 5 minutes, slowly drizzle 1 cup of water from the sides of the pan with the help of a ladle. Water added at this stage will bring down the temperature of the sugar syrup and will not allow it to boil and break the grey layer.

4. Continue to simmer the syrup over a medium flame for about 10 minutes and then gently remove the grey layer using a slotted spoon.

5. Bring the syrup to the boil once again and then slowly drizzle another cup of water from the sides of the pan using a ladle. Remove all the remaining impurities from the syrup, again using a slotted spoon.

6. Increase the flame and boil vigorously for 1 to 2 minutes. Keep aside.

HOW TO PROCEED

1. Mix 2 teaspoons of the plain flour with ¾ cup of water to make a flour solution. Keep aside.

2. Heat the sugar syrup in a deep pan over a high flame and allow it to boil vigorously.

3. When it boils, sprinkle half the flour solution in the sugar syrup and then add the chenna balls by upturning the plate on which they are kept. (Do not touch the chenna balls at this point as they are fragile).

4. When the flour solution is added, a frothy layer is formed on the surface of the syrup.

5. If the frothy layer begins to subside, sprinkle the remaining half portion of the flour solution.

6. After this, keep on sprinkling water (minimum 1 cup) on the surface of the sugar syrup. Ensure that the syrup froths all the time while cooking the rasgullas.

7. Cook for about 15 minutes, continuously sprinkling water to enable the froth to form.
8. Check if the rasgullas are cooked. This is determined by touch. If the rasgulla springs back and retains its shape when pressed, it is cooked. Another way of checking is to drop a rasgulla in a pan of cold water. If it sinks to the bottom, it is cooked.
9. Remove from the fire.
10. Transfer the rasgullas to a bowl along with 2 ladles of sugar syrup and 1 cup of water.
11. Cool and chill for approx. 3 to 4 hours before serving.

- Rasgullas should always be cooked on a very high flame.
- While cooking rasgullas, the sugar syrup must froth continuously.
- The pan should be approximately 200 mm. (8") in diameter and 150 mm. (6") in height and the sugar syrup should fill about ⅓ of the pan.
- While making rasgulla shapes (see variations on page 17), always ensure that there are no cracks on the surface of the shapes.
- While cooking, rasgullas expand to at least 4 times their original size.
- While sprinkling water on the syrup when the rasgullas are cooking, make sure you sprinkle a little water at a time (approx. a teaspoon at a time using your hands) and not large quantities.
- The cooking time of the rasgullas will vary depending on their size (i.e. large shapes viz. the rolls, rajbhog etc. will need more cooking time and vice versa).

Variation : KAMALA BHOG

Add a few drops of orange essence (or 1 teaspoon of finely chopped orange rind) and a few drops of orange food colour to the chenna and proceed as for rasgullas. Also, add a few drops of orange food colour to the sugar syrup just before adding the chenna balls to it.

Variation : RASGULLA SHAPES

SQUARES :
Divide the chenna into 14 equal portions
and gently shape each portion into
a 25 mm. x 25 mm. (1" x 1") square.

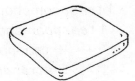

LOGS :
Divide the chenna into 8 equal portions and
gently roll each portion into the shape of a log
of 12 mm. (½") diameter and 50 mm. (2") length.

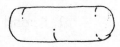

Proceed with the sugar syrup and the method of cooking as stated in the
preceding recipe.
Use as required.

RAJ BHOG

Picture on page 51

Saffron flavoured rasgullas stuffed with dry fruits.
Another popular variation of the rasgullas.

Preparation time : 30 mins.   Cooking time : 40 mins.
Makes 8 pieces.

FOR THE RAJ BHOGS
1 recipe chenna, page 128
a few drops saffron food colour

1 teaspoon plain flour (maida) for dusting

TO BE MIXED INTO A STUFFING

1 tablespoon chenna, page 128
1 teaspoon chopped pistachios
1 teaspoon chopped almonds
½ teaspoon sugar
5 strands saffron
½ teaspoon cardamom powder

FOR THE SUGAR SYRUP

5 cups sugar
½ cup milk

OTHER INGREDIENTS

2 tablespoons plain flour (maida)

FOR THE RAJ BHOGS

1. Knead together the chenna and saffron food colour and divide into 8 equal portions. Keep aside.
2. Divide the stuffing into 8 equal portions. Keep aside.
3. Flatten each portion of the chenna gently between the palms of your hands to make circles of 50 mm. (2") diameter.
4. Place one portion of the stuffing in each circle and bring the ends together to seal the edges on top.
5. Shape the stuffed raj bhogs into rounds by rolling them gently between the palms of your hands and taking care to see that there are no cracks on the surface.
6. Place the raj bhogs on the back of a flat plate (thali) which is lightly dusted with flour.

FOR THE SUGAR SYRUP

1. Combine the sugar and milk with 3 cups of water in a large pan approx. 200 mm. (8") in diameter and 150 mm. (6") in height and heat while stirring continuously till the sugar dissolves. When the syrup comes to a boil, the impurities in the sugar will begin to float on the surface, forming a grey layer.
2. Heat over a medium flame to allow the grey layer to float. Do not stir at this point as the layer will break and it will not clarify the syrup.

3. After about 5 minutes, slowly drizzle 1 cup of water
from the sides of the pan with the help of a ladle. Water added
at this stage will bring down the temperature of the sugar syrup and
will not allow it to boil and break the grey layer.
4. Continue to simmer the syrup over a medium flame
for about 10 minutes and then gently remove the grey layer
using a slotted spoon.
5. Bring the syrup to the boil once again and then slowly drizzle
another cup of water from the sides of the pan using a ladle.
Remove all the remaining impurities from the syrup,
again using a slotted spoon.
6. Increase the flame and boil vigorously for 1 to 2 minutes.
Keep aside.

HOW TO PROCEED

1. Mix 2 teaspoons of the plain flour with ¾ cup of water to
make a flour solution. Keep aside.
2. Heat the sugar syrup in a deep pan over a high flame and
allow it to boil vigorously .
3. When it boils, sprinkle half the flour solution
in the sugar syrup and then add the raj bhogs by
upturning the plate on which they are kept.
(Do not touch the raj bhogs at this point as they are fragile).
4. When the flour solution is added, a frothy layer is formed
on the surface of the syrup.
5. If the frothy layer begins to subside, sprinkle the remaining
half portion of the flour solution.
6. After this, keep on sprinkling water (minimum 1 cup) on the surface
of the sugar syrup. Ensure that the syrup froths
all the time while cooking the raj bhogs.
7. Cook for about 20 minutes, continuously sprinkling water
to enable the froth to form.

8. Check if the raj bhogs are cooked. This is determined by touch. If the raj bhog springs back and retains its shape when pressed, it is cooked. Another way of checking is to drop a raj bhog in a pan of cold water. If it sinks to the bottom, it is cooked.

9. Remove from the fire.

10. Transfer the raj bhogs to a bowl along with 2 ladles of sugar syrup and 1 cup of water.

11. Cool and chill for approx. 3 to 4 hours before serving.

- Raj bhogs should always be cooked on a very high flame.
- While cooking the raj bhogs, the sugar syrup must froth continuously.
- The pan should be approximately 200 mm. (8") in diameter and 150 mm. (6") in height and the sugar syrup should fill about ⅓ of the pan.
- When sprinkling water to the syrup when the raj bhogs are cooking, make sure you sprinkle a little water at a time (approx. a teaspoon at a time using your hands) and not large quantities.

Variation : BADAM BHOG

Use 2 teaspoons of chopped almonds instead of pistachios and almonds for the above recipe. When the badam bhogs are chilled, squeeze and drain the syrup from the badam bhogs and dip them in rabdi cream, page 129. Lift each bhog out with a fork, tap out the excess rabdi cream and place in paper cups. Garnish with slivered almonds and varq. Serve chilled.

RASMADHURI

Picture on page 25

Rasgulla rolls interlaced with sandesh and attractively presented banana leaf boats.

Preparation time : 30 mins.   No cooking.   Makes 8 pieces.

8 rasgulla logs, page 17

OTHER INGREDIENTS
1 recipe sandesh, page 120
5 strands saffron, soaked in 1 tablespoon milk
1 tablespoon chopped nuts (almonds, pistachios)
¼ teaspoon cardamom (elaichi) powder
3 tablespoons milk
2 fresh banana leaves

FOR THE GARNISH
1 tablespoon pistachio slivers
2 drops saffron food colour

1. Make 8 banana leaf boxes as shown
in the diagram on page 22. Keep aside.
2. Make rasgulla logs as stated in the recipe on page 17.
Drain the syrup and slit the rasgulla logs vertically
into 2 equal parts. Keep aside.
3. Divide the sandesh into 2 equal parts.

4. In one portion of the sandesh, add the saffron milk,
chopped nuts and cardamom powder and mix well.
Divide into 8 portions. Keep aside.
5. To the other sandesh portion, add the milk and mix well
to make a smooth mixture.
6. Sandwich one portion of the saffron-sandesh mixture
between two parts of each rasgulla log and
place in a banana leaf box.
7. Top each box with the sandesh-milk mixture
so as to completely fill the box and smoothen
the upper surface with the back of a knife.
8. Garnish with the pistachios slivers and
lines of saffron colour as shown in the picture on page 25.
Serve chilled.

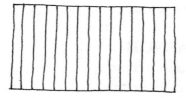
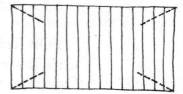

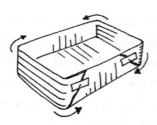

LYCHEE SANDWICH

Fresh fruit rasgulla sandwiches –
a delicacy which will just melt in your mouth.

Preparation time : 20 mins.   No cooking.   Makes 7 pieces.

14 rasgulla squares, page 17

TO BE MIXED INTO A FILLING
3 tablespoons chopped lychee
2 tablespoons rabdi cream, page 129

FOR THE GARNISH
½ cup rabdi cream, page 129
3 drops yellow food colour
7 lychee halves

FOR THE RASGULLA SQUARES
1. Make the rasgulla squares as mentioned in the recipe on page 17.
Remove the chilled rasgulla squares from the syrup and
squeeze out the excess syrup.
2. Place a rasgulla square on a plate and spread a spoonful of
the filling on it. Sandwich with another rasgulla square.
3. Repeat for the remaining rasgulla squares and
filling to make 6 more rasgulla sandwiches.
4. Place a lychee half on top of each lychee sandwich.
5. Mix the rabdi cream with the yellow food colour and fill it into
a piping bag fitted with a star nozzle.
6. Garnish the sides of the lychee sandwich
by piping a border with the rabdi cream.
Serve chilled.

Variation : PEACH SANDWICH
Use chopped peaches instead of lychees for the above recipe.

KESAR RASMALAI

Picture on facing page

Rasgulla discs soaked in sweetened saffron flavoured milk.
Next to rasgullas, this is the most popular Bengali sweet outside Bengal.
A well made rasmalai well melt in your mouth.

Preparation time : 30 mins.   Cooking time : 1 hour.
Makes 16 rasmalai.

FOR THE RASGULLA DISCS
1 recipe chenna, page 128
1 teaspoon plain flour (maida)
for dusting

FOR THE SUGAR SYRUP
5 cups sugar
½ cup milk

FOR THE SAFFRON FLAVOURED MILK
1 litre full fat milk
¼ cup sugar
a few saffron strands, dissolved in milk
¼ teaspoon cardamom (elaichi) powder

OTHER INGREDIENTS
2 teaspoons plain flour (maida)

FOR THE GARNISH
2 tablespoons slivered pistachios

FOR THE RASGULLA DISCS
1. Divide the chenna into 16 equal portions and gently shape
each portion into a flat round (disc) of 25 mm. (1") diameter
and 6 mm. (¼") thickness. Take care to see that
there are no cracks on the surface.
2. Dust the back of a flat plate (thali) lightly with
the flour and place the chenna discs on it.

1. Rasmadhuri, *page 21*
2. Gulab, *page 30*
3. Kesar Rasmalai, *above*

24

FOR THE SUGAR SYRUP

1. Combine the sugar and milk with 3 cups of water
in a large pan approximately 200 mm. (8") in diameter
and 150 mm. (6") in height and heat while
stirring continuously till the sugar dissolves.
When the syrup comes to a boil,
the impurities in the sugar will begin
to float on the surface, forming a grey layer.
2. Heat over a medium flame to allow the grey layer to float.
Do not stir at this point as the layer will break and
it will not clarify the syrup.
3. After about 5 minutes, slowly drizzle 1 cup of water
from the sides of the pan with the help of a ladle.
Water added at this stage will bring down
the temperature of the sugar syrup and
will not allow it to boil and break the grey layer.
4. Continue to simmer the syrup over a medium flame
for about 10 minutes and then gently remove
the grey layer using a slotted spoon.
5. Bring the syrup to the boil once again and
then slowly drizzle another cup of water from
the sides of the pan using a ladle.
Remove all the remaining impurities from the syrup,
again using a slotted spoon.
6. Increase the flame and boil vigorously for 1 to 2 minutes.
Keep aside.

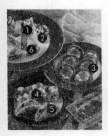

FOR THE SAFFRON FLAVOURED MILK

1. Heat the milk in a broad non-stick pan and bring it to a boil. Add the sugar, saffron milk and cardamom powder and mix well.
2. Remove from the fire.

FOR THE RASGULLA DISCS

1. Mix 2 teaspoons of the plain flour with ¾ cup of water to make a flour solution. Keep aside.
2. Heat the sugar syrup in a deep pan over a high flame and allow it to boil vigorously.
3. When it boils, sprinkle half the flour solution in the sugar syrup and then add the chenna discs by upturning the plate on which they are kept. (Do not touch the chenna discs at this point as they are fragile).
4. When the flour solution is added, a frothy layer is formed on the surface of the syrup.
5. If the frothy layer begins to subside, sprinkle the remaining half portion of the flour solution.
6. After this, keep on sprinkling water (minimum 1 cup) on the surface of the sugar syrup. Ensure that the syrup froths all the time while cooking the rasgulla discs.
7. Cook for about 15 minutes, continuously sprinkling water to enable the froth to form.
8. Check if the rasgullas are cooked. This is determined by touch. If the rasgulla springs back and retains its shape when pressed, it is cooked. Another way of checking is to drop a rasgulla disc in pan of cold water. If it sinks to the bottom, it is cooked.
9. Remove from the fire.
10. Transfer the rasgullas to a bowl along with 2 ladles of sugar syrup and 1 cup of water.
11. Cool and chill for approximately 3 to 4 hours.

HOW TO PROCEED

1. Remove the rasgulla discs from the sugar syrup and squeeze out the excess syrup.
2. Place the discs in a serving bowl and top with the hot saffron flavoured milk.
3. Chill for at least 2 hours.
Serve garnished with slivered pistachios.

Variation : MANGO RASMALAI

In the above recipe, add ¼ cup mango purée to the saffron flavoured milk. Garnish with fresh mango slices.

Variation : ANGOORI RABDI

Divide the chenna into 36 equal parts and shape each portion into a ball. Proceed as per the above recipe. Also use quick rabdi, page 114, instead of the saffron flavoured milk.

GULAB

Picture on page 25

Make this attractive sandesh rose and show off your culinary skills.

Preparation time : 15 mins.   No cooking.   Makes 7 pieces.

7 rasgulla discs (rasmalai), page 24

FOR THE GARNISH
1 recipe sandesh, page 120
2 edible silver leaves (varq)
2 tablespoons milk
1 to 2 drops rose essence
3 tablespoons pistachio powder
a few saffron strands

1. Make the rasgulla discs as mentioned in the recipe on page 24.
Remove the chilled rasgulla discs from the syrup and
squeeze out the excess syrup.
2. Cover one side of each rasgulla disc with the silver leaf.
3. Mix together the sandesh, milk and rose essence till
it is smooth and no lumps remain.
4. Make a layer of petals along the sides of each rasgulla disc
with the sandesh mixture using a flat teaspoon
as shown in the diagram on page 31.
5. Fill the centre with pistachio powder and saffron.
Serve chilled.

 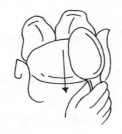 

CHUM CHUM

These tear drop shaped rasgullas have a firmer texture as
they are cooked in a thicker sugar syrup.

Preparation time : 30 mins.   Cooking time : 50 mins.
Makes 8 pieces.

FOR THE CHUM CHUMS
1 recipe chenna, page 128
2 to 3 drops saffron food colour
1 teaspoon plain flour (maida) for dusting

FOR THE SUGAR SYRUP
5 cups sugar
½ cup milk
¼ teaspoon saffron food colour

OTHER INGREDIENTS
2 teaspoons plain flour (maida)
½ cup desiccated coconut

FOR THE CHUM CHUMS

1. Knead together the chenna and food colour and
divide the mixture into 8 equal parts. Keep aside.
2. Flatten each portion between the palms of your hands and
shape them into ovals, taking care to see that
there are no cracks on the surface.
3. Dust the back of a flat plate (thali) lightly with the flour and
place the chum chums on it.

FOR THE SUGAR SYRUP

1. Combine the sugar and milk with 3 cups of water in a large pan
approx. 200 mm. (8") in diameter and 150 mm. (6") in height and
heat while stirring continuously till the sugar dissolves.
When the syrup comes to a boil, the impurities in the sugar will begin
to float on the surface, forming a grey layer.
2. Heat over a medium flame to allow the grey layer to float.
Do not stir at this point as the layer will break and
it will not clarify the syrup.
3. After about 5 minutes, slowly drizzle ½ cup of water from
the sides of the pan with the help of a ladle.
Water added at this stage will bring down the temperature of the
sugar syrup and will not allow it to boil and break the grey layer.
4. Continue to simmer the syrup over a medium flame
for about 10 minutes and then gently remove the grey layer
using a slotted spoon.
5. Bring the syrup to the boil once again and then slowly
drizzle another ¼ cup of water from the sides of the pan
using a ladle. Remove all the remaining impurities in the syrup,
again using a slotted spoon.
6. Add the saffron colour, increase the flame and boil vigorously
for 1 to 2 minutes. Keep aside.

HOW TO PROCEED

1. Mix 2 teaspoons of the plain flour with ¾ cup of water to make a flour solution. Keep aside.
2. Heat the sugar syrup in a deep pan over a high flame and allow it to boil vigorously.
3. When it boils, sprinkle half the flour solution in the sugar syrup and then add the chum chums by upturning the plate on which they are kept. (Do not touch the chum chums at this point as they are fragile).
4. When the flour solution is added, a frothy layer is formed on the surface of the syrup.
5. When the frothy layer begins to subside, sprinkle the remaining half portion of the flour solution.
6. After this, keep on sprinkling water (minimum 1 cup) on the surface of the sugar syrup. Ensure that the syrup froths all the time while cooking the chum chums.
7. Cook for about 15 minutes, continuously sprinkling water to enable the froth to form.
8. Check if the chum chums are cooked. This is determined by touch the chum chum springs back when touched and retains its shape when pressed, it is cooked. Another way of checking is to dip a chum chum in a pan of cold water. If it is sinks to the bottom, it is cooked.
9. Increase the flame to high so that the sugar syrup thickens and cook for 5 more minutes.
10. Remove from the fire.
11. Transfer the chum chums to a bowl along with 3 ladles of sugar syrup and 1 cup of water.
12. Allow the chum chums to cool completely about 3 to 4 hours. Remove the chum chums from the syrup and squeeze out the excess syrup.

13. Roll the chum chums in desiccated coconut so as to evenly coat them.
Serve chilled.

- Chum chums should always be cooked on a very high flame.
- While cooking chum chums, the sugar syrup must froth continuously.
- The pan should be approximately 200 mm. (8") in diameter and 150 mm. (6") in height and the sugar syrup should fill about $\frac{1}{3}$ of the pan.
- While sprinkling water on the syrup when the chum chums are cooking, make sure you sprinkle a little water at a time (approx. a teaspoon at a time using your hands) and not large quantities.

QUICK
DRY FRUIT
MITHAI

KAJU PISTA ROLL

Cylindrical rolls of cashewnut barfi stuffed with pistachios.

Preparation time: 15 mins.　　No cooking.　　Makes 14 rolls.

⅓ recipe pista barfi, page 131
1 recipe cashew barfi, page 130

OTHER INGREDIENTS
ghee for greasing

FOR THE GARNISH
4 edible silver leaves (varq)

1. Make the pista barfi as specified in the recipe on page 131.
2. Divide into two equal parts and
shape each portion into a cylindrical roll of 100 mm. (4") length
and 6 mm. (¼") thickness. Keep aside.
3. Make the cashew barfi as specified in the recipe on page 130.
4. Divide into 2 equal parts. Roll out each portion
with the help of a greased rolling pin on a sheet
of plastic to a rectangle of 100 mm. x 75 mm. (4" x 3")
and 3 mm. (1/8") thickness.
5. Place one portion of the pistachio roll on one side
of the cashewnut rectangle.
6. Roll out tightly starting from the end where the pistachio roll is
placed and seal the edges completely.
7. Gently press the roll till it is about 175 mm. (7") length.
8. Roll this onto 2 silver leaves so it coats the
kaju pista roll completely.
9. Cut into 7 pieces of 25 mm. (1") each.
10. Repeat for the remaining ingredients to make 1 more roll.

AKHROT
CHOCO TARTS

Delicious tarts made with walnut barfi topped with
a creamy chocolate topping.

Preparation time : 10 mins.   Cooking time : 25 mins.   Makes 10 tarts.

FOR THE WALNUT BASE
½ cup (50 grams) walnuts, coarsely powdered
¼ cup (25 grams) cashewnuts, coarsely powdered
¼ cup (50 grams) sugar
oil to grease

FOR THE CHOCOLATE TOPPING
½ cup (60 grams) grated
   dark chocolate
¼ cup (50 grams) cream

FOR THE GARNISH
5 walnut halves, cut into two

1. Dissolve the sugar in 4 to 5 tablespoons of water and simmer
   to get a syrup of 1 string consistency (refer page 8).
2. Add the walnuts and cashewnuts and mix well. Heat over a slow
   flame and stir till it leaves the sides of the pan.
3. Remove from the fire, transfer to another plate and
   cool completely.
4. Divide the mixture in 10 equal portions.
Press each portion into 25 mm. (1") diameter greased tart moulds.
5. Unmould the tarts and keep aside.

FOR THE TOPPING

1. Heat the cream in a pan and bring it to a boil. Add the chocolate and mix well to get a smooth sauce, making sure that no lumps remain.
2. Cool completely. Pour into a piping bag fitted with a star nozzle and keep aside.

HOW TO PROCEED

1. Pipe a swirl of the topping into each walnut tart, using a piping bag.
2. Garnish with the walnut pieces.

• **If you do not want to make tarts, you can also roll the mixture into a square and cut small pieces of the barfi.**

PISTA KAJU SANDWICH

Picture on page 26

Pista barfi sandwiched with dry fruits and flavoured with saffron and cardamom.

Preparation time : 30 mins.   Cooking time : 10 mins.
Makes 8 pieces.

1 recipe pista barfi, page 131
ghee for greasing

FOR THE FILLING

3 tablespoons sugar
½ cup chopped dry fruits (almonds, cashewnuts, walnuts)
3 tablespoons powdered cashewnuts
a few saffron strands
¼ teaspoon cardamom (elaichi) powder

FOR THE GARNISH
edible silver leaves (varq)
a few saffron strands, dissolved in milk

1. Make the pista barfi as specified in the recipe on page 131.
2. Divide the mixture into 2 equal portions.
3. Roll out each portion with the help of a greased rolling pin on a sheet of plastic into a 125 mm. (5") diameter circle and keep covered.

FOR THE FILLING
1. In a pan, combine the sugar with 4 tablespoons of water and simmer to get a syrup of 1 string consistency (refer page 8).
2. Add all the other ingredients and mix well for 2 to 3 minutes. Keep aside to cool.

HOW TO PROCEED
1. Place one pista barfi circle on a plate and spread the filling mixture evenly on it.
2. Top with the second pista barfi circle and allow to set for 20 to 30 minutes.
3. Cover with silver varq and cut the sandwich into 8 wedges.

DILPASAND BARFI

Picture on page 26

A delectable combination of figs, cashew and pistachio barfis,
rolled to create this tricolour Swiss roll.

Preparation time : 10 mins.   No cooking.   Makes 8 slices.

½ recipe anjeer barfi, page 132
½ recipe cashew barfi, page 130
2 tablespoons broken cashewnuts
½ recipe pista barfi, page 131

poppy seeds (khus khus) for coating

1. Make the anjeer, cashew and pista barfi as mentioned
in the respective recipes on pages 132, 130 and 131.
2. Roll out the anjeer barfi into a rectangle
of 100 mm. x 150 mm. (4" x 6").
3. Add the broken cashewnuts to the cashew barfi and mix well.
4. Roll out the cashew barfi into a rectangle
of 87 mm. x 150 mm. (3½" x 6").
Place this on top of anjeer rectangle.
5. Roll out the pista barfi into a cylindrical roll of 150 mm. (6") width
and 12 mm. (½") thickness.
6. Place the pista barfi roll on one side of the anjeer-cashew rectangle.
7. Roll tightly starting from the end where the pista barfi roll
is placed and seal the edges completely.
8. Gently press the roll till it is about 200 mm. (8") long.
9. Roll this onto poppy seeds so that the poppy seeds coat
the barfi completely.
10. Cut the roll into 8 slices of 25 mm. (1") thickness.

PISTA PAAN

A cone made of pistachio barfi filled with gulkand flavoured dry fruits.

Preparation time : 20 mins.   No cooking.   Makes 8 pieces.

1 recipe pista barfi, page 131

TO BE MIXED INTO A FILLING
1 tablespoon powdered sugar
1 tablespoon pistachios, blanched, peeled and chopped
2 tablespoons almonds, blanched, peeled and chopped
2 tablespoons gulkand
1 tablespoon poppy seeds (khus khus)
¼ teaspoon cardamom (elaichi) powder
a few saffron strands

FOR THE GARNISH
3 edible silver leaves (varq)

1. Make the pista barfi as specified in the recipe on page 131.
2. Roll out this dough in between 2 sheets of plastic till
it is 6 mm. (¼") thick. Cut 8 squares of 75 mm. x 75 mm. (3" x 3 ")
each (re-roll the scrap if required).
3. Keep these squares covered with plastic till required.
4. Divide the filling into 8 equal portions.
5. Place a portion of the filling diagonally on each pista barfi square.
6. Shape each square into a cone, by bringing the opposite ends
together as shown in the diagram below.
7. Cover the pista cone completely with the silver leaf.
8. Repeat for the remaining filling and pista barfi squares
to make 7 more paans.

  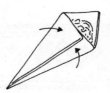

FRESH PINEAPPLE KATLI

Fresh fruit barfi cooked with cashewnuts in a light sugar syrup.

Preparation time : 10 mins.   Cooking time : 15 mins.
Makes 16 pieces.

½ cup cooked pineapple purée, page 43
½ cup sugar
¾ cup powdered cashewnuts
¼ teaspoon cardamom (elaichi) powder
a few saffron strands

OTHER INGREDIENTS
ghee for greasing

FOR THE GARNISH
slivered pistachios

1. Combine the pineapple purée and sugar in a pan and cook on a very slow flame till the sugar has dissolved while stirring continuously.
2. Add the cashewnuts, cardamom powder and saffron and continue cooking till the mixture leaves the sides of the pan, while stirring continuously.
This will take approximately 5 to 7 minutes.
If the katli is very sticky, cook for a further 2 to 3 minutes.
3. Pour the mixture onto a greased surface.
Roll out into a 100 mm. x 100 mm. (4" x 4") square.
4. Decorate with the slivered pistachios and cut into 25 mm. x 25 mm. (1" x 1") squares. Allow it to cool completely.

- To get pineapple purée, cook ½ cup finely chopped pineapple with 3 tablespoons of water for about 5 minutes and then purée in a food processor.

Variation : FRESH SITAPHAL KATLI
Use ½ cup cooked custard apple purée (deseeded) instead of the pineapple for the above recipe.

KAJU BADAM TACOS
Picture on page 26

Almond taco shells stuffed with a cashew filling. A sweet version of the famed Mexican tacos.

Preparation time : 15 mins.   No cooking.   Makes 8 tacos.

1 recipe badam barfi, page 130
1 recipe cashew barfi, page 130
2 tablespoons broken cashewnuts
a few drops yellow food colouring
a few saffron strands
2 to 3 slivered pistachios

1. Make the badam barfi and cashew barfi as mentioned in the respective recipes on page 130.
2. Divide the badam barfi into 8 equal portions and roll out each portion between 2 sheets of plastic into circles of 100 mm. (4") diameter. Keep aside.
3. Add the broken cashewnuts and yellow food colouring to the cashew barfi and mix well. Divide into 8 equal portions and shape each portion into a cylinder 100 mm. (4") long and 25 mm. (1") thickness.

4. Place one cashew barfi cylinder in the centre of the badam barfi circle and fold over to form a semi circle like a taco.
5. Repeat for the remaining ingredients to make 7 more tacos.
6. Garnish with slivered pistachios and saffron and serve.

BADAM PISTA BASKET

Picture on page 26

Almonds and pistachios make delightful mithai baskets.

Preparation time : 15 mins.   No cooking.   Makes 6 baskets.

1 recipe badam barfi, page 130
½ recipe pista barfi, page 131
a few drops yellow food colouring
4 edible silver leaves (varq)

1. Make the badam barfi and pista barfi as mentioned in the respective recipes on page 130 and 131.
2. Add the yellow food colouring to the badam barfi and mix well.
3. Divide the badam barfi into 6 equal portions. Shape each portion to make a flower pot as shown in the above diagram.
4. Divide the pista barfi into 8 equal portions.
5. Shape 6 pista barfi portions into rounds. Shape the rest of the pista barfi into a 150 mm. (6") long roll with 3 mm. (1/8") thickness. Cut the roll into 6 nos. 25 mm. (1") long pieces.
6. Stuff the badam flower pots with the 6 pista barfi rounds.
7. Decorate the flower pots with a pista roll handle to form a basket.
8. Garnish with the silver leaves and scraps of the badam barfi as shown in the above diagram.

BADAMI MATKI

Picture on page 26

Almond barfi shaped to resemble small earthenware containers.

Preparation time : 15 mins.   No cooking.   Makes 6 pieces.

1 recipe badam barfi, page 130
2 edible silver leaves (varq)
a few drops yellow food colouring
2 to 3 pistachio, slivered

1. Make the badam barfi as mentioned in the recipe on page 130.
2. Divide the badam barfi into two portions, ²⁄₃ and ¹⁄₃.
3. To the ²⁄₃ portion, add the yellow food colouring and mix well.
4. Divide into 6 equal portions.
5. Shape each portion into the shape of a matki
(as shown in the diagram below).
6. Roll out the remaining ¹⁄₃ portion of the barfi into
a sheet of 6mm. (¼") thickness.
Cut with heart shaped cookie cutters to get 18 heart-shaped pieces.
7. Cover each matki with 3 heart-shaped pieces
(as shown in the diagram below).
8. Garnish with a sliver of pistachio and cover the base of
the handi with the silver leaves.

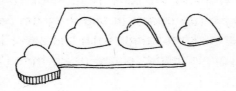

CHEQUERED BARFI

Picture on page 26

Almond, pistachio and cashewnut barfi layered attractively.

Preparation time : 15 mins.   No cooking.   Makes 8 pieces.

1 recipe badam barfi, page 130
1 recipe cashew barfi, page 130
1 recipe pista barfi, page 131
a few saffron strands
1 tablespoon milk
4 to 5 edible silver leaves (varq)

1. Make the badam, cashew and pista barfis as mentioned
in the respective recipes on pages 130 and 131.
2. Dissolve the saffron in the milk, add it to the cashew barfi and mix well.
3. Divide the badam barfi, cashew barfi and pista barfi into
3 equal portions.
4. Roll out each portion into a cylinder of 200 mm. (8") length
and 6 mm. (¼") thickness.
5. On a sheet of plastic, place one badam roll, one cashew roll and
one pista roll next to each other, to form a layer.
6. Top the first layer with a cashew roll, pista roll and
badam roll (in that order).
7. Top with the third layer of pista roll, badam roll and cashew roll.
8. Press gently so that all the barfi rolls stick together to form a
rectangle. (as shown in the diagram below)
9. Garnish the rectangle with the silver leaves.
10. Cut the rectangle into 8 slices of 25 mm. (1") thickness.

   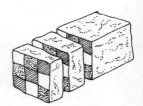

HEALTHY
HALWAS

ANJEER HALWA

A sumptuous halwa to which the addition of ground almonds
lends a smooth texture.

Preparation time : 10 mins.   Cooking time : 20 mins.   Serves 4.

24 nos. (200 grams) dried figs (anjeer)
3 tablespoons ghee
½ cup almonds, blanched, peeled and powdered
⅓ cup milk powder
4 tablespoons sugar
¼ teaspoon cardamom (elaichi) powder

FOR THE GARNISH
2 tablespoons slivered almonds

1. Cook the figs in boiling water for about 3 to 5 minutes.
Drain and purée them in a food processor. Keep aside.
2. Heat the ghee in a heavy bottomed pan, add the powdered
almonds and sauté over a medium flame for about 2 minutes.
3. Add the puréed figs, milk powder, sugar with ½ cup of water and
cook for about 5 minutes till the sugar has dissolved,
stirring continuously.
4. Add the cardamom powder and mix well.
Serve hot, garnished with slivered almonds.

MOONG DAL SHEERA

A classic recipe of a delicious sweet.

Preparation time : 10 mins.   Cooking time : 40 mins.   Serves 4 to 6.

1 cup yellow moong dal (split yellow gram)
1 cup milk, warmed
1¼ cups sugar
½ teaspoon cardamom (elaichi) powder
a few saffron strands
6 tablespoons ghee

FOR THE GARNISH
2 tablespoons almonds and pistachios, slivered

1. Soak the moong dal in water for 3 to 4 hours.
2. Drain and grind to a coarse paste using very little water.
3. Dissolve the saffron in 1 tablespoon of warm milk and keep aside.
4. Melt the ghee in a broad non-stick pan.
5. Add the moong dal paste and stir the mixture continuously on a low flame till it becomes golden brown.
6. Add in the warm milk and 1 cup of warm water and cook, stirring continuously till all the moisture has been absorbed.
7. Add the sugar and cook on a slow flame till the ghee separates.
8. Add the saffron and cardamom powder and mix well.
9. Garnish with slivers of almonds and pistachio. Serve hot.

• **If the moong dal paste has excess water after grinding, drain it out through a strainer.**

GAJAR KA HALWA

An easy to make recipe of halwa made without using khoya.

Preparation time : 5 mins.   Cooking time : 15 mins.   Serves 4.

6 medium red carrots, grated
½ cup full fat milk
½ cup sugar
¼ teaspoon cardamom (elaichi) powder
a few saffron strands
2 tablespoons cream
3 teaspoons ghee

FOR THE GARNISH
2 tablespoons slivered almonds

1. Heat the ghee in a broad non-stick pan and
sauté the carrots for 2 to 3 minutes.
2. Add the milk and stir till it evaporates.
3. Then add the sugar and continue stirring until
the mixture is slightly thick.
4. Add the cardamom powder,
saffron (dissolved in a little milk) and cream and stir well.
Serve hot, garnished with the slivered almonds.

- **You can also make Doodhi ka Halwa in the same manner.**

50

DOODHI KA HALWA

A traditional recipe of bottle gourd cooked with milk and cardamom.

Preparation time : 10 mins.   Cooking time : 50 mins.   Serves 4.

3 cups grated doodhi (bottle gourd)
3 cups full fat milk
3 cardamoms
½ cup sugar
a few drops of green food colour (optional)
3 tablespoons ghee

FOR THE GARNISH
2 tablespoons slivered almonds

1. Heat the ghee in a pan, add the grated doodhi and
sauté till it turns translucent.
2. Add the milk and cardamoms and bring to a boil.
3. Simmer for 30 to 35 minutes, stirring occasionally.
4. When the halwa is almost dry, add the sugar and
food colour and mix well.
5. Stir for 5 to 10 minutes till the moisture has evaporated.
6. Serve hot, garnished with the slivered almonds.

Variation : DOODHI KA HALWA (SUGAR FREE)
At step 3, add 8 to 10 sachets of artificial sweetner instead of the sugar.

1. Petha Paan and Petha Slices, *page 90*
2. Kesar Petha Paan, *page 91*
3. Angoori Petha, *page 89*
4. Angoori Petha Pieces, *page 90*

53

COCONUT SHEERA

A dessert made of coconut milk.

Preparation time : 5 mins.   Cooking time : 1 hour.   Serves 4.

2 ½ cups coconut cream
1 litre full fat milk
½ cup sugar
5 cardamom (elaichi) pods, crushed
¼ cup chopped cashewnuts

OTHER INGREDIENTS
ghee for greasing

1. Soak the cashewnuts in hot water for about 10 minutes.
Drain and keep aside.
2. Mix together the coconut cream and milk and simmer in
a non-stick pan, stirring continuously.
3. When it reduces to half, add the sugar and continue simmering
on a low flame stirring continuously till it thickens and
leaves the sides of the pan and resembles khoya.
4. Add the cardamom and cashewnuts and mix well.
5. Pour into a serving bowl and refrigerate.
Serve chilled.

DESI FLAVOURED ICE-CREAMS AND KULFI

PAAN ICE-CREAM

Picture on page 51

All the goodness of ice-cream flavoured with paan. A digestive dessert.

Preparation time : 15 mins.   Cooking time : 10 mins.   Serves 8 to 10.

1 litre full fat milk
1½ cups (300 grams) sugar
¼ cup (20 grams) cornflour
1½ cups (300 grams) cream

FOR THE PAAN FLAVOURING

4 nos. Calcutta paan leaves (betel leaves)
juice of 1 lemon
6 nos. kharek, soaked overnight
1 tablespoon Lukhnowi saunf (fennel seeds), powdered
¼ teaspoon cardamom (elaichi), crushed
¼ cup gulkand
a pinch menthol

FOR THE PAAN FLAVOURING

1. Wash the paan leaves and grind them into a fine paste
along with the lemon juice in a food processor.
Sieve through a strainer and keep the juice aside.
2. Deseed and finely chop the kharek.
3. Mix together the paan juice, kharek, saunf, cardamom and
gulkand in a bowl. Keep aside.

HOW TO PROCEED

1. Dissolve the cornflour in ¼ cup of cold milk. Keep aside.
2. Place the rest of the milk in a heavy bottomed pan and bring it to a boil. Add the sugar and simmer for 5 minutes.
3. Add the dissolved cornflour and simmer for another 5 minutes while stirring continuously, till it is of a coating consistency.
4. Remove from the fire and allow it to cool completely.
5. Add the paan flavouring mixture and cream to the milk.
6. Mix well and pour into a shallow freezer proof dish.
7. Freeze till slushy. Remove and beat with a whisk until smooth and creamy. Add the menthol and mix well.
8. Freeze again until firm for about 4 to 6 hours.

- **Lucknowi saunf is smaller in size as compared to fennel seeds and more fragrant. It is available at most grocery stores and paan vendors.**

THANDAI ICE-CREAM

Creamy, smooth and heavenly.

Preparation time : 15 mins.   Cooking time : 10 mins.   Serves 8 to 10.

1 litre full fat milk
1½ cups (300 grams) sugar
¼ cup (20 grams) cornflour
1½ cups (300 grams) cream
a few saffron strands

TO BE GROUND FINELY FOR THE THANDAI FLAVOURING

¼ cup almonds
2 tablespoons poppy seeds (khus khus)
2 tablespoons Lucknowi saunf (fennel seeds)
½ teaspoon cardamom (elaichi) powder
20 nos. white peppercorns

HOW TO PROCEED

1. Dissolve the cornflour in ¼ cup of cold milk. Keep aside.
2. Dissolve the saffron in 2 tablespoons of warm milk. Keep aside.
3. Place the rest of the milk in a heavy bottomed pan and bring it to a boil. Add the sugar and simmer for 5 minutes.
4. Add the dissolved cornflour and simmer for another 5 minutes while stirring continuously, till it is of a coating consistency.
5. Remove from the fire and allow it to cool completely.
6. Add the thandai flavouring to the milk. Strain the mixture through a sieve.
7. Add the cream and dissolved saffron to the milk mixture. Mix well.
8. Pour the mixture into a shallow freezer proof dish and freeze till slushy.
9. Remove and whisk until smooth and creamy.
10. Freeze again until firm for about 4 to 6 hours.

KESAR MALAI KULFI

Rich, creamy, ice-cream made with reduced milk,
flavoured with saffron and cardamom.

Preparation time : 10 mins.　　Cooking time : 45 mins.　　Makes 5 kulfis.

1 litre full fat milk
⅓ cup sugar
¼ teaspoon cardamom (elaichi) powder
a few saffron strands
1 tablespoon arrowroot or cornflour

1. In a small bowl, soak the saffron in a little warm milk and
keep aside.
2. Dissolve the arrowroot in 2 tablespoons of water and keep aside.
3. Put the milk in a broad non-stick pan and bring it to a boil.
Add the arrowroot solution and sugar and mix well.
4. Simmer over a medium flame, stirring continuously till the milk
reduce to a little less than half the original quantity
(approximately 450 ml.).
5. Cool completely and add the cardamom powder and
saffron mixture and mix well.
6. Pour into kulfi moulds and freeze overnight till it sets.
7. To unmould, allow the moulds to remain outside the refrigerator
for 5 minutes and then unmould by inserting a wooden skewer stick
or a fork, in the centre of the kulfi and pulling it out.

Variation : GULAB JAMUN KULFI, *Picture on page 51*
* **Add 4 meva batis (recipe on page 112) to the kulfi at step 6.
Pour into jelly moulds and freeze overnight till it sets.
Unmould and slice to serve.**

ROSE AND TENDER COCONUT ICE-CREAM

Ice-cream delicately flavoured with rose petals and tender coconut.

Preparation time : 15 mins.   Cooking time : 10 mins.   Serves 4.

FOR THE ICE-CREAM
1 litre full fat milk
1½ cups (300 grams) sugar
¼ cup (20 grams) cornflour
1½ cups (300 grams) cream

FOR THE FLAVOURING MIXTURE
2 red roses
2 tender coconuts
7 to 8 drops rose essence

FOR THE FLAVOURING MIXTURE
1. Clean and finely chop the rose petals.
2. Discard the coconut water and chop the tender flesh.
3. Combine the rose essence, rose petals and coconut in a bowl. Keep aside.

HOW TO PROCEED
1. Dissolve the cornflour in ¼ cup of cold milk. Keep aside.
2. Place the milk in a heavy bottomed pan and bring it to a boil. Add the sugar and simmer for 5 minutes.
3. Add the dissolved cornflour, simmer for another 5 minutes while stirring continuously.
4. Remove from the fire and allow it to cool completely.
5. Add the flavouring mixture and cream to the milk.
6. Mix well and pour into a freezer proof dish and freeze till slushy.

7. Remove and beat with a whisk until smooth and creamy.
8. Freeze again until firm for about 4 to 6 hours.

- **Select the tender coconut carefully. The flesh should be neither be too soft nor too firm.**

CHIKI ICE-CREAM

Almond and pistachio praline flavour this ice-cream.

Preparation time : 15 mins.   Cooking time : 20 minutes.   Serves 4.

FOR THE ICE-CREAM
½ litre full fat milk
½ cup sugar
2 tablespoons cornflour
¼ teaspoon
cardamom (elaichi) powder
a few saffron strands
¾ cup cream

FOR THE CHIKI
½ cup sugar
¼ cup chopped pistachios
¼ cup chopped almonds
oil to grease

FOR THE ICE-CREAM
1. In a small bowl, soak the saffron in a little warm milk and keep aside.
2. In a pan, combine the milk, sugar and cornflour and mix well so that no lumps remain.
3. Bring to a boil stirring continuously. Simmer over a slow flame till the mixture coats the back of a spoon.
4. Add the cardamom powder and saffron mixture and mix well.

5. Cool completely. Add the cream and mix well.
6. Transfer into a freezer proof dish and freeze for 6 to 8 hours till it is slushy.

FOR THE CHIKI

1. Put the sugar in a pan and heat over a medium flame till it melts and caramelises to a light brown colour (refer page 8).
2. Remove from the flame, add the almonds and pistachios and mix well.
3. Pour onto a greased marble surface.
4. When it has cooled, break into small pieces and keep aside.

HOW TO PROCEED

1. Remove the semi-set ice-cream from the freezer and transfer it into a blender.
2. Add half the crushed chiki and blend till it is smooth and no crystals remain.
3. Transfer into the freezer proof dish, add in the remaining half of the chiki and mix well.
4. Freeze again till it sets completely.

QUICK
MITHAI

BESAN LADDU

These laddus are popular all over North India.

Preparation time : 5 mins.   Cooking time : 10 mins.   Makes 7 laddus.

¾ cup (100 grams) Bengal gram flour (besan), coarsely ground
¾ cup (100 grams) powdered sugar
⅓ cup (60 grams) ghee
¼ teaspoon cardamom (elaichi) powder
2 to 3 drops saffron colour

1. Mix together the sugar and saffron colour and keep aside.
2. Melt the ghee in a kadhai, add the gram flour and cook over a low flame stirring continuously till it is golden brown in colour.
3. Add the cardamom powder and mix well.
4. Remove from the fire and pour onto a plate (thali).
Cool completely.
5. Mix together the gram flour mixture and sugar.
6. Divide into 7 equal portions and shape into laddus.

- **You can use regular gram flour instead of the coarsely ground gram flour for the above recipe.**

KOPRA PAK

A traditional coconut sweet which is a popular favourite.

Preparation time : 20 mins.   Cooking time : 15 mins.
Makes 20 pieces.

2 cups grated fresh coconut
2 cups sugar
1 teaspoon lemon juice
a few saffron strands
1 teaspoon milk
¼ teaspoon cardamom (elaichi) powder
2 teaspoons ghee

FOR THE GARNISH
5 pistachios, blanched, peeled and cut into slices

1. Warm the milk in a small bowl, add the saffron and rub in until the saffron dissolves.
2. Dissolve the sugar with 1 cup of water and bring it to a boil. Add the lemon juice.
3. Remove the floating dirt using a slotted spoon and strain the syrup if necessary.
4. Boil the syrup again until it is of 2 string consistency (refer page 8).
5. Add the coconut, ghee, prepared saffron and cardamom powder. Remove from the fire while stirring continuously.
6. Spread the mixture on a thali (flat metal plate) and allow to cool.
7. Decorate with the pistachios. Cut into desired shape.

MOCK GULAB JAMUN

Bread koftas filled with a creamy khoya mixture, deep fried and then soaked in sugar syrup.

Preparation time : 15 mins.   Cooking time : 20 mins.
Makes 6 jamuns.

FOR THE MOCK GULAB JAMUNS
6 slices of bread
3 tablespoons grated khoya (mava), page 132
2 tablespoons chopped dry fruits (almonds, cashewnuts, pistachios)
1 tablespoon sugar
¼ teaspoon cardamom (elaichi) powder
a few saffron strands

FOR THE SUGAR SYRUP
1 cup sugar
½ cup water

OTHER INGREDIENTS
oil or ghee for deep frying

FOR THE SUGAR SYRUP
1. Combine the sugar and water in a pan and simmer to a syrup of 1 string consistency (refer page 8).
2. Remove from the heat and keep warm.

FOR THE MOCK GULAB JAMUNS
1. Remove the crusts from the bread slices.
2. Sprinkle a little water on each slice and flatten each slice using a rolling pan. Keep aside.

3. In a small bowl, mix together the khoya, dry fruits, sugar, cardamom powder and saffron.
Sprinkle a little water (approximately 1 teaspoon) and knead into a dough. Divide into 6 equal portions.
4. Place one khoya portion in the centre of each bread slice and bring the sides of the bread together in the centre so as to seal the filling completely.
5. Seal the ends tightly and lightly roll between your palms to form a ball. Ensure there are no cracks on the surface.
6. Deep fry in hot oil over a medium flame till the jamuns are golden brown.
7. Drain and transfer into the warm sugar syrup.
8. Allow them to soak the syrup for 5 to 7 minutes and drain. Serve warm topped with quick rabdi, page 114, if desired.

MALPUAS

An instant version of the traditional sweet.

Preparation time : 5 mins.   Cooking time : 20 mins.
Makes 12 malpuas.

FOR THE MALPUAS
1 cup (200 grams) cream
4 tablespoons plain flour (maida)
ghee for frying

FOR THE SAFFRON SYRUP
1 teacup sugar
a few saffron strands
2 teaspoons milk
2 teaspoons rose water (optional)

FOR THE GARNISH
2 tablespoons chopped dry fruits

FOR THE MALPUAS

1. Mix the cream and flour into a batter.

2. Smear very little ghee on a frying pan and spread
a small amount of the batter on it.

3. Fry on both sides using a little ghee until golden brown.
Drain on absorbent paper.

FOR THE SAFFRON SYRUP

1. Dissolve the sugar in 1 cup of water and simmer for 5 minutes to
make a syrup of 1 string consistency (refer page 8).

2. Warm the milk in a small bowl, add the saffron and rub until the
saffron dissolves. Add to the syrup.

3. Add the rose water and keep the syrup warm.

HOW TO PROCEED

1. Soak the malpuas in the warm saffron syrup
for 2 to 3 minutes and drain.

2. Garnish with dry fruits.
Serve warm.

PEACH HALWA

A fresh fruit dessert flavoured with nutmeg and cardamom which is also low in calories.

Preparation time : 10 mins.   Cooking time : 15 mins.   Serves 4.

2 cups peaches, peeled and finely chopped
¼ cup whole milk powder
2 tablespoons sugar
¼ teaspoon nutmeg powder (jaiphal)
¼ teaspoon cardamom seeds
a few saffron strands
2 teaspoons ghee

1. Melt the ghee in a kadhai, add the peaches and stir over a slow flame till they are soft (about 5 to 7 minutes).
2. Sprinkle the milk powder and sugar and stir continuously on a low flame till the mixture leaves the sides of the kadhai.
3. Remove from the fire, add the nutmeg powder and mix well.
4. Garnish with the cardamom seeds and saffron.
Serve hot.

• **The amount of sugar added will vary depending on the sweetness of the peaches.**

Variation : PEACH HALWA (SUGAR FREE), *Picture on page 103*
At step 2, you can use 2 teaspoons of artificial sweetner instead of sugar.

KAJU KOPRA SHEERA

Picture on page 77

Cashewnuts and fresh coconut sweetened with sugar and flavoured with cardamom and saffron.

Preparation time : 10 mins.   Cooking time : 15 mins.   Serves 4.

1 cup (100 grams) cashewnuts, coarsely powdered
1 cup grated coconut
¾ cup sugar
¼ teaspoon cardamom (elaichi) powder
a few saffron strands
4 tablespoons ghee

FOR THE GARNISH
4 to 6 cashewnuts

1. Heat the ghee in a heavy bottomed pan and sauté the cashewnuts and coconut in it for 7 to 10 minutes over medium heat, stirring continuously. The mixture should be very lightly browned.
2. Add the sugar with ½ cup of water and cook till the sugar has dissolved (approx. 5 minutes).
3. Add the cardamom and saffron and mix well.
4. Serve warm, garnished with cashewnuts.

Variation : KAJU KOPRA SHEERA (SUGAR FREE)
Use 8 to 10 sachets of artificial sweetener instead of sugar for the above recipe.

RICE KHEER

Picture on page 104

A quick and easy recipe. A great way to use left-over rice.

Preparation time : 5 mins.   Cooking time : 15 mins.   Serves 4.

1 cup cooked rice
2 cups milk
1/3 cup condensed milk
2 tablespoons sugar
1/2 teaspoon cardamom (elaichi) powder
1 teaspoon ghee

1. Mix together the rice, milk and condensed milk in a broad
non-stick pan and simmer on a low flame,
stirring continuously, for about 10 minutes.
2. Add the sugar, cardamom powder and ghee and mix well
till the sugar has dissolved.
Serve hot.

• **The rice should be over cooked to get a more creamy texture
for the kheer.**

Variation : RICE KHEER (SUGAR FREE)
Use 4 to 6 sachets of artificial sweetner, instead of the sugar.

SITAFAL FIRNI

Milk thickened with rice flour and flavoured with custard apple.

Preparation time : 15 mins.   Cooking time : 20 mins.   Serves 4.

1 litre full fat milk
4 tablespoons rice flour
4 to 6 tablespoons sugar
1½ cups custard apple (sitafal) pulp, deseeded

1. Make a smooth paste using the rice flour and ½ cup of cold milk.
2. Mix this in the remaining milk and sugar and bring to a boil over
a medium flame, stirring continuously.
3. Simmer for 5 to 10 minutes till the mixture thickens and
the rice flour is cooked.
4. Cool completely and add the custard apple pulp.
5. Mix well and chill for 3 to 4 hours.
Serve chilled.

INSTANT JALEBIS

A quick variation of the traditional dessert using yeast to ferment the jalebis instantly.

Preparation time : 10 mins.   Cooking time : 15 mins.   Makes 15 jalebis.

FOR THE JALEBI BATTER
1 cup plain flour (maida)
1 teaspoon
Bengal gram flour (besan)
½ teaspoon fresh yeast, crumbled
1 tablespoon melted ghee
1 teaspoon sugar
2 to 3 drops of lemon
yellow food colouring

FOR THE SUGAR SYRUP
½ cup sugar
a few saffron strands
¼ teaspoon lemon juice

OTHER INGREDIENTS
ghee for deep frying

FOR THE JALEBI BATTER
1. Sieve the plain flour and gram flour together.
2. Dissolve the yeast in 1 tablespoon of water.
3. Mix the flour mixture, yeast solution, ghee, sugar and lemon yellow food colouring with ⅔ cup of water to make a thick batter, making sure that no lumps remain.
4. Keep aside for 10 minutes till the yeast ferments.

FOR THE SUGAR SYRUP
1. Dissolve the sugar in ½ cup of water and simmer for 5 minutes till the syrup is of 2 string consistency (refer page 8).
2. Add the saffron and lemon juice and mix.
3. Remove from the fire and keep aside.

HOW TO PROCEED

1. Heat the ghee in a broad saucepan
[the ghee should be approximately 25 mm. (1") deep].
2. Fill the jalebi batter into a piping bag with a single hole nozzle or
a thick cloth with a small hole in the centre which is
finished with button-hole stitch.
3. Press out round whirls of the batter into the hot ghee
working closely from outside to the centre of the whirl
[approx. 50 mm (2") diameter].
4. Deep fry the jalebis till golden brown and transfer into
the warm sugar syrup.
5. Drain immediately and serve hot.

* **Do not allow the jalebi batter to overferment.
Fry the jalebis immediately once the batter has rested for 10 minutes.**

ELABORATE MITHAI

MYSORE PAK

This delicious fudge from South India has a granular texture.
Do not be alarmed by the amount of ghee mentioned in the recipe
as most of it is drained out at the end of the cooking process.

Preparation time : 10 mins.   Cooking time : 20 mins.
Makes 12 pieces.

⅓ cup (50 grams) Bengal gram flour (besan)
⅓ cup (50 grams) plain flour (maida)
½ cup melted ghee
¾ cup (150 grams) sugar

FOR POURING INTO THE FLOUR MIXTURE
3 cups melted ghee, hot

1. In a bowl, combine the gram flour, plain flour and
melted ghee and mix well. Keep aside.
2. In a kadhai, dissolve the sugar in ¼ cup of water and bring to
a boil. Simmer till the syrup is of 1 string consistency (refer page 8).
3. Add the gram flour mixture and mix well, stirring continuously in
one direction, over a medium flame.
4. Pour the hot ghee a little at a time (approximately ¼ cup) from
a height so that it trickles in a thin stream in the centre of the
Mysore pak mixture.
5. Stir continuously in a circular motion on a low flame. When the
ghee is absorbed, the Mysore pak mixture will increase in volume
(expand). Stir in one direction (clockwise or anti-clockwise) only.
When the mixture settles down a little, pour more
hot ghee again and stir in the same manner.

1. Kaju Kopra Sheera, *page 70*
2. Ghevar, *page 83*
3. Quick Rabdi, *page 114*

6. Repeat steps 4 and 5 till the entire quantity of 3 cups of ghee has been poured and absorbed by the Mysore pak mixture.

7. Sprinkle ½ teaspoon of cold water on the Mysore pak. If it is ready, the Mysore pak will sizzle indicating that it is ready to be poured out.

8. Pour the mixture into a tray or thali approximately 100 mm. (4") in diameter. The sides of the thali should be at least 50 mm. (2") high.

9. Allow it to set and harden for about 5 minutes.
Then, crack a small hole and drain out all the excess ghee.
Approximately 2 to 2½ cups will get drained out.

10. Cut into 12 squares and store in an air-tight container.

- **If a colander is used instead of the tray or thali to set the Mysore pak, keep a bowl under the colander to collect the excess ghee which will drain out automatically.**

KAJU MYSORE PAK

Delicate honeycombs of cashewnuts, a true delicacy that simply melts in the mouth. Making this requires your full attention.

Preparation time : 15 mins.   Cooking time : 20 mins.   Makes 12 pieces.

⅓ cup (50 grams) cashewnuts, powdered
⅓ cup (50 grams) plain flour (maida)
½ cup melted ghee, warm
½ teaspoon cardamom (elaichi) powder
¾ cup (150 grams) sugar

1. Amrit Peda, *page 100*
2. Pista Roll, *page 100*
3. Mava Anjeer Roll, *page 109*
4. Mava Kesar Roll, *page 108*
5. Milk Cake, *page 96*

79

FOR POURING INTO THE FLOUR MIXTURE
3½ cups melted ghee, hot

1. In a bowl, combine the cashewnuts, flour, ghee and
cardamom powder and mix well. Keep aside.

2. In another pan, combine the sugar with ⅓ cup of water
and bring to a boil.
Simmer till the syrup is of 1 string consistency (refer page 8).
Add the cashewnuts and flour mixture and mix well,
over a slow flame, stirring in one direction.

3. Pour the hot ghee, a little at a time from a height so that it
trickles in a thin stream into the cashewnut mixture.
Keep stirring with a ladle in a clockwise direction, adding larger
quantities of the ghee towards the end.

4. When the Mysore pak expands and some ghee separates,
sprinkle ½ teaspoon of cold water on the pak. If it is ready, the
Mysore pak will sizzle indicating that it is ready to be poured out.

5. Pour the mixture into a tray or a thali
approximately 100 mm. (4") in diameter.
The sides of the thali should be at least 50 mm. (2") high.

6. Allow it to set a little. Then, crack a small hole on one side and
drain out all the excess ghee.
Approximately 2 to 2½ cups will get drained out.

7. Cut into 12 squares and store in an air-tight container.

CHURMA LADDU

Churma is a traditional Rajasthani sweet, made specially during festivities. Churma is the powdered form which is also made into laddus.

Preparation time : 15 mins.   Cooking time : 45 mins.
Makes 10 laddus.

1½ cups (200 grams) whole wheat flour (gehun ka atta),
coarsely ground
¼ cup grated dry coconut (copra)
2 tablespoons sesame seeds (til)
¾ cup (150 grams) jaggery, grated
2 tablespoons ghee

OTHER INGREDIENTS
ghee for deep frying
poppy seeds (khus khus) for coating the laddus

1. Make a stiff dough of the whole wheat flour using ½ cup of water. Knead very well.
2. Divide the dough into 8 equal portions.
3. Shape the portions into the shape of your fist and press with your fingers in the centre of each portion to make an indentation as shown in the diagram on page 82.
4. Heat ghee in a large kadhai and deep fry the dough portions on a very slow flame for approximately 25 to 30 minutes until they are golden brown in colour.
5. Drain on absorbent paper and allow them to cool.
6. Pound in a mortar and pestle to coarse pieces. Grind the pieces further in a food processor to get a fine powder (churma).

7. Heat 1 tablespoon of ghee in a pan,
add the grated coconut and sesame seeds and sauté
for about 2 minutes. Remove and keep aside.
8. Heat the jaggery with the remaining tablespoon of
ghee and 1 tablespoon of water on a medium flame till
the jaggery dissolves. Cool slightly.
9. Mix the ground churma, coconut and sesame seeds with
the melted jaggery.
10. Allow the mixture to cool slightly.
11. Divide into 10 portions and shape into rounds.
Roll each laddu in poppy seeds.
Store the laddus in an air-tight container.

GHEVAR

Picture on page 77

A filigreed Rajasthani delicacy made with the help of a mould.

Preparation time : 10 mins.   Cooking time : 2 hours.
Makes 25 small ghevars.

1¾ cups (200 grams) plain flour (maida)
1 tablespoon (10 grams) arrowroot or cornflour
¼ cup melted ghee, cooled
1 recipe sugar syrup, page 87 (lavang latika)
a few drops of kewda essence

OTHER INGREDIENTS
ghee for deep frying

1. Combine the flour, arrowroot and melted ghee in a bowl.
2. Add 1 cup of water in a thin stream, whisking continuously
taking care to see that an emulsion is formed and
the water and ghee do not separate.
3. Add 2 more cups of water again in a thin stream while whisking
continuously. At no point should the ghee and water separate.
4. The batter should be of a coating consistency. More water can be
added if required to achieve the required consistency.
5. Keep the batter in a cool place away from the heat.
6. Place the ghevar mould in a kadhai and pour melted ghee in it till it
reaches ¾ of the height of the mould.
7. Remove 2 ladles of the batter at a time into a small bowl and
place it near the gas range.

8. Heat the ghee on a medium flame and put in one spoonful of the batter into the mould in a thin stream. The batter should settle in the mould.
9. When the froth subsides, pour in another spoonful in the centre in a thin stream.
10. Repeat seven times making a hole in the centre of the ghevar using a wooden skewer stick. Pour the batter into this centre each time.
11. Increase the flame and allow it to cook in the centre by pouring ladlefuls of hot ghee in the centre of the mould 2 or 3 times.
12. When the centre is firm and cooked, pull the ghevar out gently, by inserting a wooden skewer in the centre and pulling it out of the ghee.
13. Immerse in sugar syrup, drain quickly and place on a serving plate.
14. Repeat steps 7 to 13 and use the remaining batter to make 25 ghevars.

- You have to buy a special ghevar mould to make this delicacy. You can also use a primus stove ring of size 4 [75 mm. (3") in diameter] to obtain 25 ghevars. Alternatively, you can use a larger mould to get fewer ghevars in which case the cooking time will increase.

Serving suggestion :
You can also top the ghevar with quick rabdi, page 114.

MOHANTHAAL

A classic recipe of a delicious sweet.

Preparation time : 10 mins.   Cooking time : 60 mins.
Makes approx. 20 pieces.

1 cup ghee
2 cups coarsely ground Bengal gram flour (besan)
1 cup grated khoya (mava), page 132
1 teaspoon cardamom powder (elaichi)

FOR THE SUGAR SYRUP

1½ cups sugar
1 cup water
2 tablespoons milk

FOR THE GARNISH

4 tablespoons chopped
almonds and pistachios

1. Place the gram flour in a bowl.
2. Heat the ghee and pour half of it over the gram flour.
3. Rub the ghee into the gram flour till
the mixture resembles bread crumbs.
4. Put the remaining hot ghee in a kadhai, add the gram flour mixture
and cook till the mixture is golden brown, stirring continuously.
5. Add the grated khoya and cardamom powder and stir for
about 5 to 7 minutes.
6. Remove from the heat and allow to cool till it is warm.

FOR THE SUGAR SYRUP

1. Mix the sugar with water in a pan and simmer for 10 minutes.
2. Add the milk to the boiling sugar syrup.

3. The impurities will from a grey layer.
Remove this layer gently using a slotted spoon.
4. Simmer this till the syrup is of 1 string consistency (refer page 8).
Keep the syrup hot.

HOW TO PROCEED
1. Pour the hot sugar syrup over the cooked
gram flour mixture and stir well.
2. Pour into a greased 225 mm. (9") diameter thali
with 25 mm. (1") high sides.
3. Sprinkle chopped almonds and pistachios on top
and allow to set for 4 to 5 hours.
4. Cut into 25 mm. (1") squares.
Serve at room temperature.

LAVANG LATIKA

Sweetened khoya and dry fruits encased in a crisp pastry and
sealed with a clove.

Preparation time : 10 mins.   Cooking time : 30 mins.
Makes 12 pieces.

FOR THE COVERING
1 cup plain flour (maida)
3 tablespoons ghee, melted

TO BE MIXED INTO A FILLING

3 tablespoons
grated khoya (mava), page 132
2 tablespoons chopped dry fruits
1 tablespoon sugar
¼ teaspoon
cardamom (elaichi) powder
a few saffron strands

FOR THE SUGAR SYRUP

1 cup sugar
½ cup water

OTHER INGREDIENTS

12 cloves
ghee for frying

FOR THE SUGAR SYRUP

1. Combine the sugar and water in a pan and simmer till it reaches a 1 string consistency (refer page 8).
2. Remove from the heat and keep warm.

FOR THE COVERING

1. Combine the flour and ghee in a bowl and make a stiff dough using enough water. Knead well.
2. Divide the dough into 12 equal portions.
3. Roll out each portion into a circle of 125 mm. (5") diameter.

HOW TO PROCEED

1. Place 1 tablespoon of the filling at one end of the circle. Fold the ends (as shown in the diagram below) and seal the edges using a little water.
2. Insert a clove on top of the sealed edge.
3. Deep fry in ghee over a slow flame until golden brown in colour.
4. Remove and drain on absorbent paper.
5. Soak the lavang latikas in warm sugar syrup for about 2 to 3 minutes.
6. Drain and serve warm.

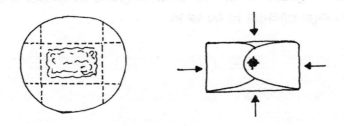

PETHA

White pumpkin cooked in sugar syrup is a delicacy from Agra in North India where this variety of pumpkin grows abundantly.

Preparation time : 30 mins.   Cooking time : 45 mins.
Makes 30 pieces.

4 kgs. white pumpkin (ash gourd or petha)
¼ teaspoon slaked lime (chuna)
3 cups sugar

1. Peel and deseed the pumpkin and cut it into 25 mm. (1") squares.
2. Prick each piece with a fork at close intervals.
3. Rub the pumpkin pieces with the slaked lime and keep them aside for 10 to 15 minutes. Wash the pumpkin pieces thoroughly. Drain and keep aside.
4. In a heavy bottomed pan, dissolve the sugar in 2 cups of water and bring to a boil.
5. Skim off any impurities floating on the surface using a slotted spoon.
6. Simmer till the syrup is of 1 string consistency (refer page 8) and add the pumpkin pieces.
7. Simmer for 10 to 15 minutes till the syrup is of 3 string consistency (refer page 8). Remove from the fire.
8. Cool completely in the sugar syrup and then drain.
9. Allow it to harden a little overnight in a cool place.
10. Store in a cool place. Petha keeps well for several days.

• **You need good quality ripe ash gourd (petha) to make this sweet. The skin of the gourd should be whitish green in colour which indicates the petha is ripe enough to be used.**

ANGOORI PETHA

Picture on page 52

A variation of the famous Agra ka Petha.

Preparation time :30 mins.   Cooking time : 30 mins.
Makes 40 pieces.

2 kg. white pumpkin (ash gourd)
¼ teaspoon slaked lime (chuna)
3 cups sugar
a few drops yellow food colour
1 cup desiccated coconut

1. Peel and deseed the pumpkin. Using a melon scoop,
   scoop out balls from the pumpkin.
2. Prick each pumpkin ball with a fork at close intervals.
3. Rub the slaked lime on the pumpkin balls and
   keep aside for 5 minutes.
4. Wash the pumpkin balls thoroughly. Drain and keep aside.
5. In a heavy bottomed pan, combine the sugar and yellow food
   colouring with 2 cups of water and bring to a boil.
6. Skim off any impurities floating on the surface,
   using a slotted spoon.
7. Add the pumpkin balls and cook on a high flame
   for 10 to 15 minutes. Remove from the fire. Cool completely.
8. Drain from the sugar syrup and roll the petha balls
   in desiccated coconut.

Variation : ANGOORI PETHA PIECES, *Picture on page 52*
Cut the pumpkin into 25 mm. (1") squares and then follow the above recipe from step 2. Do not roll in desiccated coconut.

Variation : PETHA SLICES, *Picture on page 52*
Slice the pumpkin into thin slices (approx. 15 to 20 slices) using a wafer slicer and then follow the above recipe from step 2. Do not roll in desiccated coconut.

PETHA PAAN

Picture on page 52

Thin petha slices stuffed with pistachio sandesh.

Preparation time : 30 mins.   No cooking.   Makes 20 pieces.

20 petha slices, recipe above
20 cloves for garnishing

TO BE MIXED INTO A FILLING
1 recipe sandesh, page 120
2 tablespoons pistachios, finely chopped
a few saffron strands
¼ teaspoon cardamom (elaichi) powder
2 to 3 drops green food colour

1. Prepare the petha slices as mentioned in the recipe for petha.
2. Divide the filling into 20 equal parts and shape each portion into even sized rounds.
3. Place one portion of the filling on a petha slice.

4. Fold it along the sides to form a triangle and stud it with a clove as shown in the picture on page 52.

• To slice the petha, use a sharp wafer slicer. Each slice should be at least 200 mm. x 200 mm. (4' x 4").

Variation : KESAR PETHA PAAN, *Picture on page 52*
Use yellow food colouring instead of the green food colouring in the above recipe.

PEACH IMRATIS

Crisp urad dal imratis soaked in a delectable peach-flavoured sugar syrup.

Preparation time : 10 mins.   Cooking time : 25 mins.
Makes 8 to 10 imratis.

FOR THE IMRATI BATTER
⅓ cup urad dal (skinned split black lentils)
1 tablespoon cornflour
a few drops yellow food colouring

FOR THE PEACH SUGAR SYRUP
1 cup sugar
1 cup water
4 to 5 tablespoons peach
flavoured drink

OTHER INGREDIENTS
ghee for deep frying

FOR THE IMRATI BATTER

1. Soak the urad dal in warm water for 2 to 3 hours.
2. Drain the urad dal and grind it in a food processor
along with the cornflour, yellow food colouring and
approximately ¼ cup of water to make a very fine paste.
The paste should resemble a cake batter. Add more water if required.

FOR THE SUGAR SYRUP

1. Combine the sugar and water in a pan and bring to a boil.
2. Simmer till the syrup of 1 string consistency. Remove from the fire.
3. Add the peach flavouring and mix well. Keep the syrup warm.

HOW TO PROCEED

1. Fill the imrati batter into a piping bag with
a single hole nozzle or a thick cloth with a small hole in the centre
which is finished with button-hole stitch.
You can also use a plastic ketchup bottle with a nozzle.
2. Heat ghee in shallow non-stick pan (the ghee should be
approx. 1" deep). Pipe out the batter to drop a continuous pattern of
a flower having a round centre and 7 round petals into
the hot ghee (as shown in the diagram) on a slow flame.
Deep fry the imratis on both sides until golden brown in colour.
3. Drain and soak the hot imratis into the warm sugar syrup.
Drain immediately and serve hot.

- **It will take a little practice to pipe the imratis out correctly.
Try practicing piping out the batter in a plate or a bowl till
you get it correct and then start piping the batter into the ghee.**

CHENNA MALPUA

Delicate and lacy malpuas made with fresh paneer.

Preparation time : 20 mins.   Cooking time : 30 mins.
Makes 20 malpuas.

FOR THE MALPUAS
1 cup chenna, page 128
1 cup cold milk
4 tablespoons plain flour (maida)
4 tablespoons cornflour

FOR THE SYRUP
1¼ cups (250 grams) sugar
a few drops kewda essence

OTHER INGREDIENTS
ghee for deep frying

FOR THE SUGAR SYRUP
1. Dissolve the sugar in 1 cup of water and boil for 5 minutes.
2. Cool slightly and add the kewda essence.

FOR THE MALPUAS
1. Mix the chenna, milk, plain flour and cornflour in a bowl and
make a smooth batter by blending the mixture in a blender.
2. Heat ghee in a shallow non-stick pan
(the ghee should be approx. 1" deep).
3. Pour 1 tablespoon of the batter into the ghee. It will double in size.

4. Deep fry on both sides till lightly browned.
5. Repeat for the remaining batter.

HOW TO PROCEED

1. Drain and soak the hot malpuas into the prepared sugar syrup and allow them to soak for approximately 5 minutes.
2. Drain the malpuas from the syrup and arrange them on a serving plate.
Serve warm.

BARFIS,
MILK & MAVA
BASED MITHAI

MILK CAKE

Picture on page 78

A rich cake made with thickened milk.

Preparation time : 10 mins.   Cooking time : 40 mins.   Makes 1 cake.

2 litres full fat milk
¼ teaspoon alum (phitkari)
½ cup (100 grams) sugar
40 grams ghee

FOR THE GARNISH
5 almonds, slivered
whipped cream

1. Pour the milk in a heavy bottomed non-stick pan and bring to a boil.
2. Add the alum and mix well.
3. Simmer till the milk reduces to half, stirring continuously.
4. Add the sugar and increase the flame stirring continuously, till the sugar has dissolved.
5. The mixture may appear curdled, but continue to simmer and stir till it thickens and resembles khoya.
6. Keep stirring on a high flame till all the liquid evaporates.
7. Add the ghee and mix well.
8. Meanwhile, grease a 200 mm. (8") diameter cake tin and decorate the base with the slivered almonds.
9. Pour the hot milk cake mixture on it and cover with aluminium foil.
10. Cool to room temperature and then chill.
11. Upturn the cake onto a serving plate.
Garnish with whipped cream and almonds as shown in the picture.

MALAI PEDA

Soft pedas with a grainy texture which are an all time favourite.

Preparation time : 25 mins.   Cooking time : 50 mins.
Makes 18 pedas.

1 litre full fat milk
a few saffron strands
½ cup sugar
2 pinches citric acid
4 teaspoons milk
1 level teaspoon cornflour
¼ teaspoon cardamom (elaichi) powder

FOR THE GARNISH
a few chopped almonds and pistachios

1. Boil the milk in a heavy bottomed pan,
stirring throughout, until it reduces to half.
2. Warm the saffron in a small vessel, add 2 teaspoons of milk and
rub until the saffron dissolves. Add to the boiling milk.
3. Add the sugar and cook for a further 4 to 5 minutes.
4. Mix the citric acid in 3 teaspoons of water. Add this mixture very
gradually to the boiling milk until it curdles slightly. This may require
anything from half to the entire quantity of the citric acid mixture.
5. Mix the cornflour in the balance 2 teaspoons of milk and
add to the boiling milk.
6. Continue stirring till the mixture becomes thick and
resembles khoya.

7. Add the cardamom powder and mix well. Allow to cool.
8. Shape into 18 small balls.
9. Place in paper cups, decorate with chopped almonds and pistachios and serve.

DRY FRUIT BARFI

A delicious sweet made of thickened milk and dry fruits flavoured with nutmeg and mace.

Preparation time : 15 mins.   Cooking time : 1 hour.   Serves 16 pieces.

1 litre full fat milk
2 teaspoons curds
¼ cup sugar
¼ teaspoon nutmeg (jaiphal) powder
¼ teaspoon mace (javitri) powder
¼ teaspoon cardamom (elaichi) powder
2 tablespoons chopped pistachios
2 tablespoons chopped almonds
2 tablespoons chopped figs
2 tablespoons chopped walnuts
4 drops kewra essence

1. Bring the milk to a boil in a heavy bottomed pan.
Add the curds and stir continuously on a slow flame till the milk reduces to half (approximately 30 to 35 minutes).
2. Add the sugar, nutmeg, mace, cardamom and chopped dry fruits and continue cooking on a very low flame till the milk thickens.

3. Add ¾ cup of water and keep stirring over a slow flame till all the moisture has evaporated and the mixture leaves the sides of the pan.

4. Add the kewra essence and mix well. Remove from the fire and pour into a 100 mm. x 100 mm. (4" x 4") square tin. Allow it to cool and cut in 16 squares of 25 mm. x 25 mm. (1" x 1").

• **This barfi requires slow cooking to get a brown (caramelised) colour.**

MAVA PEDA

A quick and easy sweet made of khoya and flavoured with cardamom and saffron.

Preparation time : 15 mins.   Cooking time : 15 mins.   Makes 8 pedas.

1 cup grated khoya (mava), page 132
¼ cup powdered sugar
¼ teaspoon cardamom (elaichi) powder
a few saffron strands

FOR THE GARNISH
2 to 3 slivered pistachios

1. Combine the khoya and sugar in a heavy bottomed pan and cook on a slow flame while stirring continuously till the sugar has dissolved and the mixture leaves the sides of the pan (approximately 5 to 10 minutes).

2. Remove from the fire, add the cardamom powder and saffron and mix well. Allow to cool completely.

3. Divide the mixture into 8 equal portions and shape into even sized rounds.
4. Garnish with slivered pistachios.

- **Cook the mixture on a slow flame as otherwise the ghee from the khoya will separate, giving the pedas a grainy texture.**

Variation : PISTA ROLL, *Picture on page 78*
Use a few drops of apple green colour instead of saffron. Divide this mixture into 6 equal portions and shape each portion into a roll. Garnish with silver varq and pistachio slivers.

AMRIT PEDA

Picture on page 78

Mava pedas stuffed with pistachios

Preparation time : 15 mins.   Cooking time : 15 mins.   Makes 8 pedas.

1 cup grated khoya (mava), page 132
¼ cup powdered sugar
¼ teaspoon cardamom (elaichi) powder
¼ cup pistachios, blanched, peeled and chopped
a few saffron strands

FOR THE GARNISH
2 to 3 slivered pistachios

1. Combine the khoya and powdered sugar in a heavy bottomed pan and cook on a slow flame, while stirring continuously till the sugar has dissolved and the moisture has evaporated (approximately 5 to 10 minutes).
2. Remove from the fire, add the cardamom powder and mix well. Allow it to cool completely.
3. Divide the mixture into two portions, 2/3 and 1/3.
4. In the 1/3 mixture, add the pistachios and mix well.
5. In the 2/3 mixture, add the saffron strands and mix well.
6. Divide the pistachio mixture into 8 equal portions. Shape into even sized rounds.
7. Divide the saffron mixture into 8 equal portions and shape into even sized rounds.
8. Stuff each saffron round with the pistachio round and seal the edges completely.
9. Make designs on the peda using a toothpick as shown in the picture on page 78.
10. Garnish with slivered pistachios.

PISTA CHOCO ROLL

Pistachios and chocolate make an unusual but truly divine combination.

Preparation time : 5 mins.   Cooking time : 15 mins.   Makes 15 slices.

1 cup grated khoya (mava), page 132
¼ cup powdered sugar
1 teaspoon cocoa powder
2 tablespoons chopped pistachios
2 drops rose essence

1. Combine the khoya and powdered sugar in
a heavy bottomed pan and cook on a slow flame,
while stirring continuously till
the sugar has dissolved and the moisture has evaporated
(approximately 5 to 10 minutes).
2. Cool completely, add the rose essence and mix well.
Divide into 2 equal portions.
3. In one portion, add the cocoa powder and mix well.
Roll into a 200 mm. x 75 mm. (6" x 3") rectangle.
Keep aside.
4. In the other portion, add the chopped pistachios and mix well. Make
a roll of 25 mm. (1") diameter
and 200 mm. (8") length.
5. Place the pistachio roll on the chocolate rectangle and
roll it in such a way that the chocolate rectangle covers
the pistachio roll evenly from all sides and
there are no cracks on the surface.
6. Wrap the roll in a plastic sheet or grease-proof paper and
refrigerate till firm (for approx. 10 minutes).
7. Remove the plastic sheet or grease-proof paper and
cut into 12 mm. (½") slices.

Variation : PISTA CHOCO ROLL (SUGAR FREE), *Picture on facing page*
Add 3 teaspoons of artificial sweetner instead of the sugar and proceed
as per the recipe above.

SHRIKHAND

A dessert which transforms ordinary curds into a delicacy.

Preparation time : 3 hours.   No cooking.   Serves 4.

1 kg. thick curds
¾ cup powdered sugar
a few saffron strands
1 tablespoon warm milk
2 teaspoons cardamom (elaichi) powder

FOR THE GARNISH
slivers of pistachios and almonds

1. Hang the curds in a muslin cloth in a cool place for approximately 3 hours until all the liquid (whey) has drained off.
2. Rub the saffron into the warm milk until it dissolves.
3. Mix together the hung curds, sugar, saffron mixture and cardamom in a bowl and churn using a hand blender.
4. Serve garnished with slivers of pistachios and almonds.

Variation : STRAWBERRY SHRIKHAND
Add 1 cup of sliced strawberries instead of the saffron and cardamom powder at step 3. Adjust the sugar according to the sweetness of the strawberries.

1. Lebu Sandesh, *page 121*
2. Rose Sandesh, *page 125*
3. Kesar Sandesh Bhog, *page 122*
4. Stuffed Kesar Sandesh, *page 123*
5. Mango-Vanilla Sandesh, *page 125*
6. Pineapple Sandesh, *page 124*
7. Ratabi, *page 126*
8. Rice Kheer, *page 71*

KHAREK KA HALWA

A traditional Sindhi dessert usually made in the winter.

Preparation time : 5 mins.   Cooking time : 1 hour.   Serves 4.

1 litre full fat milk
4 to 6 nos. kharek, crushed and deseeded
4 to 6 cardamoms
2 tablespoons coriander seeds (dhania)
2 tablespoons poppy seeds (khus-khus)
½ cup sugar
¼ teaspoon nutmeg (jaiphal) powder
¼ teaspoon mace (javitri) powder
3 tablespoons ghee

FOR THE GARNISH
2 tablespoons almonds, blanched and sliced
2 tablespoons pistachios, sliced

1. Put the milk in a heavy bottomed pan and bring it to a boil.
Add the kharek and cardamoms and cook on a slow flame for
about 20 to 25 minutes, stirring occasionally.
2. Roast and coarsely powder the coriander seeds.
3. Heat the ghee in another pan, add the powdered coriander seeds
and poppy seeds and sauté on a slow flame till
they turn golden brown.
4. Add this to the simmering milk and continue cooking on
a slow flame till all the moisture evaporates.

5. Add the sugar, nutmeg and mace and cook till the sugar
has dissolved.
6. Remove from the fire.
Serve hot, garnished with almonds and pistachios.

- **This can be stored in an air-tight container for upto one month in the refrigerator.**

MAVA ANJEER BARFI

This scrumptious barfi will be lapped up by even those who are not
otherwise fond of figs.

Preparation time : 10 mins.   Cooking time : 20 mins.
Makes 16 pieces.

½ cup dried figs (anjeer), chopped
1 tablespoon sugar
1¼ cups khoya (mava), grated, page 132
2 tablespoons melted ghee
¼ teaspoon cardamom (elaichi) powder

FOR THE GARNISH
1 sheet edible silver leaf (varq)

1. Heat ½ cup of water in a kadhai, add the figs and sugar and
cook on medium flame for about 5 to 7 minutes till
the sugar has dissolved.
2. Add the khoya and continue cooking,
stirring continuously till it is light brown in colour.
3. Add the ghee and cardamom powder and mix well.

4. Remove from the fire, cool and then pour onto a flat plate.
5. Shape into a 100 mm. x 100 mm. (4" x 4") square
of 12 mm. (½") thickness and garnish with varq.
6. Cut into 16 squares of 25 mm. x 25 mm. (1" x 1") and serve.

MAVA KESAR ROLL

Picture on page 78

Another variation of mava peda which resembles a Swiss roll.

Preparation time : 10 mins.   Cooking time : 10 to 12 mins.
Makes 16 slices.

2 cups grated khoya (mava), page 132
½ cup powdered sugar
¼ teaspoon cardamom (elaichi) powder
4 to 5 saffron strands, dissolved in 1 tablespoon milk
2 to 3 drops saffron food colour
2 edible silver leaves (varq)
2 to 3 slivered pistachios

1. Combine the mava and powdered sugar in a heavy bottomed pan
and cook on a slow flame, while stirring continuously till
the sugar has dissolved and the moisture has evaporated
(approximately 10 to 12 minutes).
2. Remove from the fire and divide the mixture into two equal parts.
3. Mix the cardamom powder in one part to make the mava mixture
and allow it to cool completely.
4. Add the saffron and food colour to the other part to make the
kesar mixture. Mix well and allow it to cool completely.

5. Roll out the mava mixture between two sheets of plastic to form a rectangle of 100 mm. x 150 mm. (4" x 6").

6. Roll out the kesar mixture in the same way.

7. Place the mava rectangle on a plastic sheet or cling film.

8. Place the kesar rectangle on top of the mava rectangle.

9. Carefully lift one end of the plastic sheet or cling film and roll up the mava kesar mixtures taking care to see that there are no cracks on the surface.

10. Roll cover tightly and refrigerate till firm (approx. 10 minutes) and then remove the plastic sheet or cling film.

11. Cover completely with silver leaves and cut into 16 slices.

12. Garnish each slice with slivered pistachios.

Variation : MAVA ANJEER ROLL, *Picture on page 78*

Add 4 tablespoons dried figs (anjeer), blanched and puréed to the mava mixture at step 4 in the above recipe.

GULAB JAMUN

Khoya balls fried in ghee and sweetened with saffron
flavoured sugar syrup.

Preparation time : 15 mins.   Cooking time : 45 mins.
Makes 25 jamuns.

FOR THE GULAB JAMUNS

2 cups (250 grams) hariali mava (khoya), grated
5 tablespoons plain flour (maida)
¼ teaspoon cardamom (elaichi) powder

FOR THE SUGAR SYRUP

3 cups sugar
a few strands of saffron (optional)

OTHER INGREDIENTS

ghee for deep frying

FOR THE SUGAR SYRUP

1. In a large pan, dissolve the sugar in 1½ cups of water and
bring to a boil.
2. Simmer over a slow flame till the syrup is of 1 string
consistency (refer page 8).
3. Remove any impurities which float on top of the syrup
using a slotted spoon.
4. Add the saffron and keep the syrup warm.

FOR THE GULAB JAMUNS

1. In a bowl, combine the khoya, flour and cardamom powder and
mix well. Knead into a firm dough without using any water
2. Divide this mixture into 25 equal portions and roll into rounds.
These should have no cracks on the surface as otherwise
the gulab jamuns will crack while frying.

3. Deep fry in ghee over a slow flame till the jamuns are golden brown in colour (approx. 10 to 12 minutes).
4. Drain and immerse in the warm sugar syrup. Soak for 30 minutes. Serve warm.

- **Hariali mava is a special kind of mava used to make gulab jamuns (refer page 6).**
- **The gulab jamuns should be fried in ghee for at least 10 to 12 minutes over low heat as otherwise the insides will remain uncooked.**

KALA JAMUN

Dark brown gulab jamuns coated with desiccated coconut.

Preparation time : 10 mins.   Cooking time : 45 mins.
Makes 12 pieces.

FOR THE KALA JAMUNS
2 cups (250 grams) hariali mava (khoya), grated
5 tablespoons plain flour (maida)
¼ teaspoon cardamom (elaichi) powder
2 tablespoons sugar

FOR THE SUGAR SYRUP
3 cups sugar
a few saffron strands (optional)

OTHER INGREDIENTS
ghee for deep frying
1 cup desiccated coconut

FOR THE SUGAR SYRUP
1. In a large pan, combine the sugar with 1 litre of water and bring to a boil.

2. Simmer over a slow flame till the syrup is 1 string consistency (refer page 8).

3. Remove any impurities which float on top of the syrup using a slotted spoon.

4. Add the saffron if desired and keep the syrup warm.

FOR THE KALA JAMUNS

1. In a bowl, combine all the ingredients, mix well and knead into a firm dough without using any water.

2. Divide this mixture into 25 equal portions and roll into rounds. These should have no cracks on the surface as otherwise the jamuns will crack while frying.

3. Deep fry in ghee over a medium flame till the jamuns are dark brown in colour(for approx. 10 to 12 minutes).

4. Drain and immerse in the warm sugar syrup. Soak for 30 minutes.

5. Drain and roll in desiccated coconut.

Serve at room temperature.

MEVA BATI

Picture on page 51

A richer version of gulab jamun filled with dry fruits. A great dessert for a buffet presentation.

Preparation time : 15 mins.   Cooking time : 45 mins.
Makes 24 pieces.

FOR THE GULAB JAMUNS

2 cups (250 grams) hariali mava (khoya), grated
5 tablespoons plain flour (maida)
¼ teaspoon cardamom (elaichi) powder or whole cardamom seeds

FOR THE FILLING
¼ cup chopped pistachios
¼ cup chopped almonds
1 tablespoon sugar
a few saffron strands
¼ teaspoon
cardamom (elaichi) powder

FOR THE SUGAR SYRUP
3 cups sugar
a few saffron strands (optional)

OTHER INGREDIENTS
ghee for deep frying

FOR THE SUGAR SYRUP
1. In a large pan, dissolve the sugar in 1½ cups of water and bring to a boil.
2. Simmer over a slow flame till the syrup is of 1 string consistency (refer page 8).
3. Remove any impurities which float on top of the syrup by using a slotted spoon.
4. Add the saffron if desired and keep the syrup warm.

FOR THE GULAB JAMUNS
1. In a bowl, combine all the ingredients, mix well and knead into a firm dough without using any water.
2. Divide the dough into 13 equal portions.
3. Mix one portion of the dough into the ingredients for the filling mixture and divide the filling into 12 equal portions.
4. Press out each dough portion into a circle of 50 mm. (2") and place one portion of the filling mixture in the centre.
5. Seal the filling mixture in the gulab jamun by bringing the sides together in the centre and roll gently to ensure there are no cracks on the surface.
6. Repeat to make 11 more gulab jamuns.
7. Deep fry in ghee over a slow flame till they are golden brown (approx. 10 to 12 minutes).
8. Drain and transfer into the warm sugar syrup. Soak for at least 30 minutes.

9. Drain after 10 minutes.
10. Cut each meva bati into 2 equal halves and
place on a serving plate.

Variation : CREAM MEVA BATI
The meva batis are topped with rabdi cream, page 129, and garnished with
a dot of saffron dissolved in milk and chopped pistachios.

QUICK RABDI

Picture on page 77

Milk thickened with fresh bread crumbs to give you an instant rabdi.

Preparation time : 10 mins.   Cooking time : 15 mins.   Serves 4.

2 cups milk
2 bread slices
¼ cup condensed milk
2 tablespoons sugar
¼ teaspoon cardamom (elaichi) powder
a few saffron strands

1. Remove the crusts of the bread slices and discard.
Grind the bread slices in food processor to make fresh
bread crumbs. Keep aside.
2. Bring the milk to boil in a heavy bottomed pan. Add the fresh
bread crumbs, condensed milk and sugar and cook on a high flame,
while stirring continuously (approximately 10 minutes).
3. Remove from the fire, add the cardamom powder,
saffron and mix well.
4. Refrigerate for 2 to 3 hours and serve chilled.

SUGAR FREE MITHAI

APRICOT BARFI

(SUGAR FREE)

Tangy apricots combined with dry fruits to make this mithai
which is high in fibre.

Preparation time : 10 mins.   Cooking time : 5 mins.   Makes 8 pieces.

½ cup apricot purée
⅓ cup chopped dry fruits (almonds, pistachio, cashewnuts)
1 tablespoon ghee
¼ teaspoon cardamom powder

FOR THE GARNISH
2 edible silver leaves (varq)

1. Combine all the ingredients in a bowl and knead to form a soft dough.
2. Roll out into a rectangle of 100 mm. x 50 mm. (4" x 2").
3. Garnish with varq.
4. Cut into 25 mm. x 25 mm. (1" x 1") squares.

- **To get apricot purée, blanch the apricots in hot water for 2 minutes.
Deseed and purée in a food processor.**

Variation : KHAJUR PISTA BARFI (SUGAR FREE), *Picture on page 103*
Use 1 cup black dates (deseeded and finely chopped) instead of the apricots
and chopped pistachios instead of the dry fruits.
Knead the dates till they are smooth before adding the pistachios.

PISTA BADAM KATLI

(SUGAR FREE)

Powdered almonds and pistachio sweetened with honey.

Preparation time : 10 mins.   No cooking.   Makes 16 pieces.

½ cup almonds, blanched, peeled and powdered
1 teaspoon sliced pistachios
¼ teaspoon cardamom (elaichi) powder
2 tablespoons honey
a few saffron strands

OTHER INGREDIENTS
1 teaspoon ghee for greasing

FOR THE GARNISH
1 to 2 teaspoons sliced pistachios

1. Combine all the ingredients except the ghee in a bowl and knead gently into a dough.
2. Gently roll out the dough between 2 sheets of plastic into a square of 100 mm. x 100 mm. (4" x 4").
3. Garnish with sliced pistachios and press the rolling pin over, so that they stick firmly to the katli.
4. Cut into 16 squares of 25 mm. (1") each.

• **As far as possible, use natural honey instead of the pre-packaged commercially available brands.**

DREAM ANJEER

(SUGAR FREE)
Picture on page 103

A nutritious and sumptuous fig barfi.

Preparation time : 10 mins.   Cooking time : 5 mins.   Makes 12 pieces.

12 nos. dried figs
1/3 cup chopped dry fruits (almonds, pista, cashewnuts, walnuts)
1 tablespoon ghee
¼ teaspoon cardamom (elaichi) powder
a few saffron strands

FOR THE GARNISH
2 edible silver leaves (varq)

1. Blanch the figs in boiling water for about 2 minutes.
Drain and purée them in a food processor.
2. Combine the fig purée, dry fruits, ghee, cardamom powder and
saffron to make a soft dough.
3. Roll out into a rectangle of 100 mm. x 75 mm. (4" x 3").
4. Garnish with varq.
5. Cut into 25 mm. x 25 mm. (1" x 1") squares.

EASY
SANDESH

SANDESH

A light creamy delicacy from West Bengal made with curdled milk.

Preparation time : 5 mins.   Cooking times : 10 mins.   Makes ¾ cup.

1¼ cup chenna, page 128
¼ cup sugar

1. Add the sugar to the chenna and mix gently.
2. Cook on a very low flame in a kadhai stirring continuously
with a flat wooden spoon.
3. Remove the kadhai from the flame at regular intervals
so as not to overheat the sandesh. If it does over heat,
it will become grainy and fat will separate.
4. The sandesh is ready when it leaves the sides of the kadhai
and is neither too dry not too moist.
It should have the consistency of a very soft dough.
5. The sandesh should be used immediately for making various
shapes and garnishes.

LEBU SANDESH

Picture on page 104

Lemon flavoured sandesh.

Preparation time : 10 mins.   No cooking.   Makes 6 pieces.

1 recipe sandesh, page 120
rind of 1 lemon

FOR THE GARNISH
12 strands of saffron
8 pistachios
2 to 3 drops saffron food colour, dissolved in 1 tablespoons of water

1. Grate the lemon rind and keep aside.
2. Mix together the sandesh and lemon rind and
knead well till smooth.
3. Divide into 6 equal parts and shape each piece into a shell
(shankh) using a shell mould.
4. Garnish with the saffron strands, pistachios and a dot of
saffron food colour as shown in the picture.

Variation :
Pineapple or Lychee can also be used to make other flavours of sandesh.

KESAR SANDESH BHOG

Picture on page 104

Saffron flavoured sandesh stuffed with chopped nuts.

Preparation time : 15 mins.   No cooking.   Makes 10 pieces.

1 recipe sandesh, page 120
10 to 12 strands saffron, dissolved in 2 tablespoons milk
a few drops saffron food colour
saffron strands for garnishing

TO BE MIXED INTO A STUFFING
2 tablespoons chopped pistachios
2 tablespoons chopped almonds
1 teaspoon sugar
a few saffron strands
a pinch cardamom powder

1. Divide the stuffing into 10 equal parts. Keep aside.
2. Mix together the sandesh, saffron liquid, and saffron food colour
and divide into 10 equal parts.
3. Roll out each portion into a circle of 50 mm. (2") diameter and
place one portion of the stuffing in the centre.
4. Seal the stuffing in the dough by bringing the sides together
in the centre and roll gently to ensure there are
no cracks on the surface.

5. Make slits on the upper surface of the sandesh bhog
as shown in the picture on page 104.
6. Repeat to make 9 more pieces.
Serve chilled.

Variation : STUFFED KESAR SANDESH, *Picture on page 104*
After step 4, shape the stuffed sandesh into triangles and garnish them
with saffron strands.

CHOCOLATE-VANILLA AND PEACH SANDESH

A sandesh made of three unusual flavours.

Preparation time : 10 mins.   No cooking.   Makes 10 pieces.

1 recipe sandesh, page 120
1 teaspoon cocoa powder
a few drops vanilla essence
½ teaspoon peach drink powder
1 tablespoon milk, optional

1. Make the sandesh as mentioned in the recipe.
2. Divide the sandesh into 3 equal portions.
3. To one portion, add the cocoa powder
and ½ tablespoon of milk and mix well.
4. Roll the chocolate sandesh between two sheets of
plastic into a 75 mm. X 125 mm. (3" x 5") rectangle.

5. To the second sandesh portion, add the vanilla essence and mix gently till smooth again using ½ tablespoon of milk if required.
6. Roll the vanilla sandesh between two sheets of plastic into a 50 mm. x 125 mm. (2" x 5") rectangle. Keep aside.
7. Combine the third sandesh portion with the peach drink powder and mix gently till smooth.
Roll into a 125 mm. (5") long cylinder. Keep aside.
8. Place the vanilla sandesh rectangle on the chocolate sandesh.
9. Place the peach sandesh cylinder on one side of the chocolate vanilla rectangle.
10. Roll out tightly starting from the end where the peach sandesh cylinder is placed and seal the edges completely.
11. Cover this sandesh with a plastic film and refrigerate for 4 to 5 hours.
12. Remove the plastic film and cut the sandesh into 10 slices. Serve chilled.

PINEAPPLE SANDESH

Picture on page 104

Sandesh rounds flavoured with chopped pineapple.

Preparation time : 10 mins.   No cooking.   Makes 10.

1 recipe sandesh, page 120
2 pineapple slices, finely chopped
2 to 3 drops yellow food colour

FOR THE GARNISH
a few saffron strands, soaked in 1 teaspoon milk
1 tablespoon pistachios slivers

1. Mix together the sandesh, pineapple and yellow food colour..
2. Divide into 10 equal parts and shape each portion into a patty.
3. Garnish as shown in the picture on page ... with saffron strands and slivered pistachios.
Serve chilled.

Variation : ROSE SANDESH, *Picture on page 104*

Use 3 to 4 drops of rose essence, 3 to 4 drops of rose pink food colour and 1 tablespoon of rose water instead of the pineapple slices and yellow food colour. Shape into 25 mm. x 25 mm. (1" x 1") squares. Garnish with sieved khoya (mava) and serve chilled.

MANGO-VANILLA SANDESH

Picture on page 104

Layered mango and vanilla flavoured sandesh.

Preparation time : 10 mins.   No cooking.   Makes 10 pieces.

1 recipe sandesh, page 120
2 to 3 drops mango essence
2 to 3 drops yellow food colour
2 to 3 drops vanilla essence

a few saffron strands for garnishing

1. Divide the sandesh into 2 equal parts.
2. In one part, add the mango essence and yellow food colour and mix well to make mango flavoured sandesh.
3. Line a 250 mm x 50 mm. (10" x 2") cake tin with a plastic sheet and spread an even layer of mago sandesh on it.
4. Add the vanilla essence in the other portion of the sandesh and spread an even layer over the mango sandesh.
5. Refrigerate for some time and unmould and then cut it into 10 pieces.
6. Garnish with saffron strands and serve.

RATABI

Picture in page 104

Pistachio added to sandesh gives you a mouthwatering recipe.

Preparation time : 10 mins.   No cooking.   Makes 15 pieces.

1 recipe sandesh, page 120
2 tablespoons pistachios, finely chopped
a few saffron strands
¼ teaspoon cardamom (elaichi) powder
2 to 3 drops green food colour

FOR THE GARNISHING
a few cashewnuts

1. Mix all the ingredients together to form a smooth paste.
2. Roll out the sandesh between two sheets of plastic to form a rectangle of 75 mm. x 125 mm. (3" x 5").
3. Cut into 15 pieces of 25 mm. (1") each.
4. Garnish each piece with a cashewnut.

BASIC
RECIPES

CHENNA

This is the basic ingredient used in most Bengali sweets.

Preparation time : 5 mins.   Cooking time : 10 mins.
Makes approx. 1 cup.

1 litre cow's milk
½ teaspoon citric acid (nimbu ke phoool)

1. Dissolve the citric acid in ½ cup of water and keep aside.
2. Bring the milk to a boil in a pan, stirring continuously.
3. Remove from the fire and stir for 5 to 7 minutes
till the milk is slightly cool.
4. Add the citric acid solution and stir the milk gently.
5. The milk will curdle and the whey will separate.
The whey has to be clear thus indicating the milk has completely
curdled. Allow it to rest for 3 to 4 minutes.
6. Strain out all the whey using a clean damp muslin cloth.
7. Fold all the 4 sides of the muslin cloth and twirl it gently so that
all the whey that is in the milk solids gets evenly drained out.
8. Gather the cloth from all 4 sides and squeeze the chenna lightly
about 3 to 4 times so that most of the whey gets drained out.
9. Remove the chenna onto a clean plate and knead gently
so that it is free of lumps and take care not to apply too much
pressure while kneading the chenna.
10. It is advisable to use this almost immediately.
Use as required.

Points to remember :

- Make sure that the milk is lukewarm while adding the citric acid mixture. Do not shock hot milk as it will affect the quality of the chenna.
- Always use cow's milk for making chenna as it has a low fat content. If you use buffalo's milk, let the milk rest after boiling it and then discard the skin that is formed.
- Always use fresh chenna for making rasgullas.

RABDI CREAM

This is used for garnishing various Bengali desserts.

Preparation time : 5 mins.   Cooking time : 30 mins.   Makes 1 cup.

1 litre full fat milk
2 tablespoons sugar
3 tablespoons chenna, page 128

1. Heat the milk on a medium flame in a broad non-stick pan, stirring continuously.
2. When the milk boils, add the sugar and keep stirring continuously on a medium flame till it reduces to about 1 cup.
3. Pour onto a flat plate and chill for about 20 minutes.
4. Add the chenna to it and blend in a food processor.
5. Pour again onto the flat plate and chill till it is semi-set.
Use as required.

CASHEW BARFI

Preparation time : 10 mins.   Cooking time : 20 mins.
Makes approx. 1¼ cups.

1 cup (100 grams) cashewnuts, broken
½ cup (50 grams) sugar
¼ teaspoon cardamom powder

1. Soak the cashewnuts in warm water for about 30 minutes and wash them 2 to 3 times.
2. Drain all the water out and blend the cashewnuts to a fine paste. Keep aside.
3. Dissolve the sugar in ½ cup of water and prepare a syrup of one string consistency.
4. Add the cashew paste and cook over a medium flame, stirring continuously till the mixture leaves the sides of the pan (approx. 5 to 7 minutes).
5. Transfer to a plate and cool slightly. Keep aside. Use as required.

BADAM BARFI

Preparation time : 10 mins.   Cooking time : 20 mins.
Makes approx. 1¼ cups.

1 cup (100 grams) almonds
½ cup (50 grams) sugar
¼ teaspoon cardamom powder

1. Soak the almonds in warm water for about 30 minutes.
2. Drain all the water, peel the almonds and blend them to a fine paste in food processor. Keep aside.
3. Dissolve the sugar in ½ cup of water and prepare a syrup of 1 string consistency.
4. Add the almond paste and cardamom powder and cook over a slow flame, stirring continuously till the mixture leaves the sides of the pan (approx. 5 to 7 minutes).
5. Transfer to a plate and cool slightly. Keep aside.
Use as required.

PISTA BARFI

Preparation time : 10 mins.   Cooking time : 20 mins.
Makes approx. 1¼ cups.

1 cup (100 grams) pistachios
½ cup (50 grams) sugar
¼ teaspoon cardamom powder
a few drops of green food colouring (optional)

1. Soak the pistachios in warm water for about 30 minutes.
2. Drain all the water, peel the pistachios and blend them to a fine paste in a food processor. Keep aside.
3. Dissolve the sugar in ½ cup of water and prepare a syrup of one string consistency.
4. Add the pista paste, cardamom powder and green colour and cook over a slow flame, stirring continuously till the mixture leaves the sides of the pan (approx. 5 to 7 minutes).
5. Transfer to a plate and cool slightly. Keep aside.
Use as required.

ANJEER BARFI

Preparation time : 10 mins.   Cooking time : 15 mins.   Makes ⅓ cup.

6 nos. (50 grams) anjeer (dried figs)
2 tablespoons sugar
¼ teaspoon cardamom powder

1. Purée the figs till they are broken down into very small pieces. This should measure about 1/3 cup.
2. In a pan, combine the sugar with 2 tablespoons of water and prepare a sugar syrup of 1 string consistency.
3. Add the figs and cardamom powder and cook for 4 to 5 minutes over a slow flame, stirring continuously.
4. Remove from the fire and transfer to another plate. Cool completely. Use as required.

KHOYA

A basic ingredient for various barfis.

Preparation time : 5 mins.   Cooking time : 15 mins.   Makes ¾ cup.

1 litre full fat milk

1. Heat the milk in a non-stick pan on a high flame till it comes to boil.
2. Continue simmering while stirring continuously till it becomes semi-solid.
3. Cool and use as required.